VISION INDIA 2020

Copyright © 2010 Sramana Mitra
All rights reserved.

ISBN: 1-4392-6976-9
ISBN-13: 9781439269763

VISION INDIA 2020

SRAMANA MITRA

*To the youth of India: Close your eyes,
exist in this future – be each entrepreneur.*

CONTENTS

I.	Introduction	xi
II.	Technology and Technology-Enabled Services	xix
	i. MIT India : Engineering Education	1
	ii. Lucid : K–12 education	7
	iii. Maya Ray : Rural BPO	13
	iv. Taxonomy : Software Innovation	19
	v. Convert : Software-as-a-Service (SaaS)	25
	vi. PIA : Web 3.0	31
	vii. Nucleon : Convergence Chip	35
	viii. TrueCFO : SaaS-enabled BPO	41
	ix. Equity Dispatch : Equity Research	47
III.	Infrastructure	51
	i. Green Village : Real Estate	53
	ii. Lightning Rails : Fast Trains	57
	iii. Magic Carpet Roads : Toll Roads	61
	iv. Eastgate : Ports	65
	v. Himalaya Shipping : International Shipping	71

	vi.	Gangotri : Water Desalination	77
	vii.	Mandakini : Water Diplomacy	81
	viii.	AdiShakti : Solar Energy	85
IV.	**Rural and Slum Development**		**91**
	i.	FDBI : Bank	93
	ii.	Camellia : Flower Farms	99
	iii.	Palanquin : Furniture	105
	iv.	Deepti : Candles	109
	v.	Gagori : Pottery	113
	vi.	Patami : Jute	117
	vii.	Vidyangan : Schools	121
	viii.	Amrakunja : Carbon Trading and Afforestation	125
	ix.	Him-Icon : Fruits and Vegetables	129
	x.	Cowherd Creamery : Cheese	133
V.	**Healthcare**		**139**
	i.	Harvard Medical School, India : Medical Education	141
	ii.	Doctor at Hand : Rural Pharmacies	145
	iii.	Doctor on Wire : Small-Town Hospitals	149
	iv.	Doctor for Sure : Health Insurance	153
	v.	Care : Eldercare	159
VI.	**Lifestyle Brands**		**163**
	i.	Urja : Fashion	165
	ii.	Oishi : Gifts	169
	iii.	Thakur : Gourmet Food	173
	iv.	Darjeeling : Tea Salons	177
	v.	Renaissance : Heritage Hotels	181
	vi.	Tilottama : Herbal Products	185
	vii.	Amrapali : Spa	189

CONTENTS

VII.	**Entertainment**		**193**
	i.	Elixar : Animation Film Studio	195
	ii.	Framed Ivory : Film Studio	201
	iii.	Kanishka Raja : Story Franchise	205
	iv.	Bioscope : Rural Cinema	209
	v.	NCTV : Sports	213
	vi.	Torquato Tasso : Wine Bars and Dance Clubs	217
VIII.	**Epilogue**		**221**

INTRODUCTION

Very early in my life I knew where I wanted to go. The details may have been blurry, but the direction was clear by 16 years of age: I wanted to be an entrepreneur; I wanted to study computer science in America; and finally, I wanted to write.

These were not necessarily well thought through choices, but rather instincts, born of the circumstances that surrounded and made up my particular life. Nothing esoteric, simply that my father was an entrepreneur, there was a multi-generational history of studying abroad – in England or America – and a slightly older cousin whom I looked up to had suggested that computer science was where our generation's most exciting opportunities awaited.

And so, in 1989, I left India with two dream-stuffed suitcases for college in western Massachusetts. This was long before the wave of information technology swept over India, dotting business parks across once ox-plowed fields. My Swiss Air flight roared over old Bombay, where stray cows and rickshaw traffic shrank from view.

When I arrived at Smith College in the fall of 1989, I had already made a few choices. I had chosen to attend a small liberal arts college instead of a larger engineering school like one of the IITs, Carnegie Mellon, or MIT. I did apply to MIT for undergrad, but with naïve honesty I told the man who interviewed me in Calcutta that my skills did not end with math and science. I was also a trained classical dancer, an avid watercolor painter, having studied with the renowned artist Sri Ramananda Bandopadhyay, and, heresy of heresies, that I wanted to continue indulging both my left and right brain. MIT rejected me.

Of course, this turned out to be a blessing in disguise. At Smith, I was free to indulge my natural instincts. I worked hard at computer science and economics, my two majors, programming till three in the morning, but I also managed to regularly choreograph and perform, write, take seminars in poetry and literature.

In 1992, the Smith CS department received a grant to purchase a transputer – one of the early parallel computing systems. The machine sat at the corner of the lab looking formidable and mysterious, but also rather lonely. Soon though, we were inseparable. I was the only student working on it, and I learned to dismantle it, understand it, and write programs taking advantage of its concurrency. That year, my advisor and I came up with *The Inebriated Router Algorithm*, a randomized routing algorithm for transporting traffic in multiprocessor interconnects. The resulting paper was accepted at the annual Transputer User Group meeting, and the week before my graduation in May 1993, we flew to Vancouver to present it at the conference.

This research, more than anything else, paved my way back to MIT – and back, I thought, to the office of acclaimed computer architecture professor, Anant Agarwal. But Anant remained elusive – rarely found on campus, he was deep in the throes of his first startup, Virtual Machine Works. So, I sought out a friendly senior graduate student in his group, John "Kubi" Kubiatowicz, as my mentor. I came into the Alewife project towards the end, with much of the system already designed. Kubi was its chief architect. He patiently answered all my questions as I tried to make sense of the vast number of design decisions and algorithms already arrived at. I quickly realized that at MIT, there would be minimum direct coaching, and a lot of following my nose, figuring things

INTRODUCTION

out. Sink or swim was the general idea, and I was not the sinking kind. Within a year I wrote the performance evaluation system for the Alewife multiprocessor and handed in my master's thesis based on that work.

Meanwhile, I got to know Anant better under unexpected circumstances. In January 1994, the Indian VLSI conference was in Calcutta, and Anant was one of the keynote speakers. I attended the conference with him, and one evening, I showed him around town in my 1972 Fiat. Zigzagging between bumper-to-bumper traffic, I explained to Anant my entrepreneurial aspirations. Anant, nervous about the traffic, resonated, encouraging me to keep going.

From 1994 to 2000, I founded and ran three companies – DAIS, Intarka, and Uuma. Each leveraged the Internet in unique ways, and through each I learned the essentials of the Silicon Valley venture business: building products and teams, raising money, marketing and selling vision, ideas, solutions, and companies.

But as the technology industry melted down around me, I felt the need for a broader perspective than what startup CEO jobs typically allowed. The need to focus on an increasingly narrow niche is critical to the success of a fledgling venture, yet my own personal desire at that point was promiscuity, not focus. I wanted to be a consultant rather than a proprietor. In this capacity I led turnarounds, positioning and repositioning exercises, and strategic planning efforts. My clients ranged from zero-stage startups all the way to the $10 billion SAP and the $45 billion Best Buy. All told: 15-plus years as a Silicon Valley insider, stewarding ventures big and small, newborn and matured through the vast innovation ecosystem.

In 2005, my journalist friend Om Malik baited me to start a blog. "Just do it," he said. "You're so opinionated anyway. Just write what you think. Just be you!"

When I sat down to write, words tumbled forth without effort – piling themselves up for me to sift through, cut, chop, arrange, and finally hand over to my quickly amassing audience. The blogosphere was calling. And when, in the fall of 2007, the technology editor of Forbes.com, Elisabeth Corcoran, invited me to write a weekly column, it went from calling me, to calling me home.

Soon after, in February, I wrote a controversial column titled, "The Coming Death of Indian Outsourcing." India, I said, for all its glory, remained the world's back office. Its tech industry little more than a "services" industry, where the customers did the thinking. India executed. India, I wrote, had not learned to invent technology products of its own. Barring a few exceptions, the glut of venture capital chasing India found it difficult to be deployed. There was way too much money, and way too few deals.

I stood by this thesis then, and I stand by it today. Tech-sector VCs are now diverting capital to retail, real estate, hotels, and other non-tech sectors. India's $30 billion IT/ITES services industry, meanwhile, is slowly and surely losing its competitive advantage. Most of the four million people that the industry employs have now "arrived." They have breezed through the milestones that their fathers had to toil all their lives to reach. A phone. A watch. A TV. A car. A house. For the golden goose is still laying large, warm eggs, enough to feed the four million and their families, servants, chauffeurs, and cooks. Meanwhile, the workforce is getting comfortable in their cubicle chairs, just as the turkey gets comfortable before Thanksgiving.

Of course, this is a sensitive issue that called forth a deluge of hate mail. But not hate mail alone. I also received calls from many CEOs from the Indian outsourcing industry congratulating me for having the guts to point out, albeit in scathing words, that the outsourcing industry is in troubled water.

True, India has positioned itself as a software superpower on the shoulders of outsourcing. But is that all that we will ever achieve? With the right guidance, I am resolute that the Indian youth have the potential to build their nation's next phase of development – systematic development rather than the haphazard, helter-skelter development we have thus far seen.

INTRODUCTION

Development, for India, of course, will not be limited to the technology sector. Driving from Calcutta to Kharagpur last year, I experienced intimately the toll of one of India's many unforgiving bottlenecked roadways. A highway cut to one lane because of a bridge that has stood derelict for three years. Outside Jaipur, where a thick mass of trucks constrict the flow of traffic, the scene is unchanged. And when I do finally persevere, make it home, find my bed, the noise pollution keeps sleep distant. I toss and turn in bed, listening through the walls to my family members' coughing unrest due to the environmental disaster we have created.

These same trucks that clog my journey to Jaipur are caught up in similar jams up and down the length and breadth of India. They wheeze to a halt trying to deliver goods to train stations to be transported across the heartland of India, or to ports so ships can sail.

And the people? Dripping in sweat, hanging from fuming buses, packed like sardines in trains they trudge on. Living in postage-stamp-sized slum rooms amidst squalor, crime, and health hazards, the majority of twenty-first-century India's citizens live a life far below "superpower" standards.

India needs clean water. India needs energy. India needs roads, ports, and bridges. But India also needs to look back as it strides forward.

In the name of development, India has managed to destroy much of its architectural heritage. Real estate entrepreneurs have mercilessly destroyed British-era jewels along with much of the traditional Indian heritage buildings. Such, I understand, is the destiny of developing nations. The same routine destruction runs from Kashmir to Kanyakumari. It runs in Mexico, in China. It runs in Brazil, and in Romania. Darjeeling, the erstwhile queen of the Himalayas, once enchanted with pine-lined walks strung from house to house, today flashes neon signs to welcome tourists. In the heart of the Himalayas, the picturesque villages are upgraded from utmost poverty and poetry to mediocrity. Their sun-bleached

Buddhist prayer flags that flap in the mountain wind no longer whisper their blessings. This is the era of cement, of development for development's sake.

But what of beauty? Of preservation? Paris preserved. Kyoto. San Francisco. Will India fail to preserve? Will India fail to showcase the magic and the mystique of its past? Between consulting and writing, over the last decade, I have interacted with thousands of entrepreneurs and innovators, encountering hundreds of business case studies, and from that rich crop I have harvested ideas to answer these issues.

George Will once said, "Not only do ideas have consequences, but only ideas have large and lasting consequences."

Vision India 2020 is my notebook of ideas on entrepreneurship in India. Set in 2020, this futuristic retrospective looks back on the building of a set of particular entrepreneurial ventures, gleaned from the many opportunities I see at the end of the first decade of the twenty-first century. Much, much in these ventures need yet be fleshed out. But if you start thinking about a venture in your own area of interest with the framework offered in one of these essays, I believe you will find directives – strategy, business models, references, comparables – that will guide you forward.

Whether in film or healthcare, education or rural development, I have dreamed freely, taking bold, ambitious measures to address impending crises such as water, energy, and the environment.

As you read this book, take with you that boldness. And afterwards, as your own ideas gestate, use my process of visioning – of imagining a manifestation, in as real of terms as possible, of the company that you will build, the change you will bring about.

It is a powerful experience to project far into the future – *your* future, based on *your* ideas, *your* dreams. But as you dream, be sure to work out the details requisite to your venture's success. I have envisioned details as granular as logos and colors, not to mention margins and pricing. It is within such details that billions of

INTRODUCTION

dollars of GDP await – quietly, unregistered by the greater public, waiting for an entrepreneur's magic touch. For in my model of development, it is the entrepreneurs, and the entrepreneurs alone, who wield the most potent weapons of mass reconstruction.

To build markets; to build nations; to build worlds.

TECHNOLOGY AND TECHNOLOGY-ENABLED SERVICES

MIT INDIA

Twelve years ago, in 2008, the labor arbitrage–based IT services industry, which had staked India's place in the global technology market, was facing a dire threat. The supply-demand equilibrium was failing. India's engineering education system simply could not keep up with the demand for talent. And in what talent it did supply, quality was quickly becoming an issue.

Engineering schools below the top tier (IIT, IISC, and a few others) were struggling to retain, let alone recruit faculty. Multinational companies were dangling lucrative, foreign job offers in front of anyone who knew engineering. Shuffling out to teach in an unknown engineering college at the end of a dirt road was out of the question.

Susan Hockfield was then the president of Massachusetts Institute of Technology. MIT had taken a leadership role in the OpenCourseWare (OCW) movement, posting every faculty lecture online, accessible to anybody in the world, anywhere in the world.

I had been on the advisory board of the MIT India program for several years before that and had a chance to think about MIT's India strategy. In its earlier incarnation, MIT India was a relatively low-key program, sending students as interns to be placed at various Indian companies to gain experience working in one of the two most quickly emerging economies in the world. I was not happy with the strategy of the program and had, on numerous occasions, expressed my discontent, always emphasizing that we could and should be doing a great deal more. But push as I did, I could not bring my ideas to fruition.

So, I decided to implement the MIT India strategy I had in mind as a for-profit, private company to train engineers in India.

It took a great deal of lobbying up and down the MIT management chain to convince Dr. Hockfield to take equity in the company on behalf of MIT, and even more before she let us do the project under the MIT India brand, leveraging OCW content. We would, it was understood, only grant certificates, not MIT degrees. Nonetheless, the resistance was strong since the MIT brand was a hyper-sensitive issue amongst the institute's administrators.

Gradually, I managed to enlist the support of a great many of the Indian faculty at the institute, starting with Anant Agarwal, whom I had worked with as a graduate student a decade earlier. With Anant's support I began to bring other faculty into the fold, including the legendary Arvind, Sanjoy Mitter, Anantha Chandrakasan, Srinivas Devadas, and Madhu Sudan at the department of electrical engineering and computer science, Senthil Todadri in physics, Mriganka Sur and Pawan Sinha in brain and cognitive sciences, and Abhijit Banerjee in economics. They, in turn, helped me convince Dr. Hockfield that MIT's approach to India needed a grand rethinking.

Beyond this faculty support, there were three other levers that I pushed in this process. First, the MIT alumni had no shortage of highly successful Indian entrepreneurs, including Vivek Ranadive, founder of TIBCO, Suhas Patil, founder of Cirrus Logic, Amar Bose, founder of Bose Corporation, and the list went on. The idea of making a dramatic impact on India's engineering education by leveraging the MIT teaching methodology and OCW content resonated with all of them, and as major contributors to MIT's endowment, they had their own ways of persuading the president.

Secondly, for early stage investors, I solicited venture capitalists who were also influential MIT alumni. Mark Gorenberg of Hummer Winblad, Gus Tai of Trinity Ventures, Lip Bu Tan of Walden, and Brian Jacobs of Emergence Capital each saw the potential of building a sizable venture based on the idea, and brought their firms, and their immense negotiating leverage, to the venture.

Finally, I approached my contacts in the Indian political arena to complete the onslaught of persuasion. Dr. Manmohan Singh himself led the effort, with Mr. Somnath Chatterji, then speaker of the Lok Sabha, and an old family friend who had helped me get DAIS off the ground in 1995, moving every chess piece necessary to offer the project a real chance.

Dr. Hockfield, with input from faculty, from a wide range of alumni, and enthusiastic invitations and incentives from the Indian government, began to see clearly the scope for making a tremendous multi-generational impact on India's education. She could not resist.

When we launched MIT India in 2010, we were handsomely financed by contracts from Intel, Cadence, Autodesk, Tata Motors, and IBM. In addition, companies like Cadence and Autodesk donated CAD tools over which our engineering students sweated. Intel Capital became an investor in the venture and negotiated the deal with Intel's India management. Beyond this, we worked with the extensive rolodex of our investors, board members, and government associates. Besides, Dr. Hockfield, once on board, became our most enthusiastic champion, contacting every single major engineering company operating in India on our behalf.

Our model was simple. We worked directly with major corporations interested in hiring trained engineers. Our customers, thus, were companies, not students or parents.

To the youth of India, though, we brought yet another value proposition: not only training, but guaranteed, high-caliber jobs.

To begin this process, we created a comprehensive talent scouting program to recruit students from across 5,000 high schools using an effective PR campaign that asked teachers to nominate their top students on our Web site. Each year, millions of students took the IIT entrance exams, and only a small number gained admission. Many of those left behind, and many others whose family financial constraints required them to find jobs immediately, their academic potential notwithstanding, were perfectly qualified, and we managed to attract thousands of them into our program.

These students, upon acceptance into the MIT India program, were guaranteed a job at the sponsor company for which we trained them. For example, Tata Motors had us train mechanical engineers, while Intel had us train chip designers.

The course load and schedule was intense, broken into three trimesters of four courses each, covering 24 courses in two years. Forget about summer vacation; we ran one-month breaks after each course. Each curriculum was custom designed for a specific sponsor, and sponsors could request interdisciplinary courses for a set of students in a batch (or batch after batch). For example, Genetech could ask for a computer science and biology cross-course, which would cover, per trimester, two biology and two CS courses.

Throughout the two-year period, we sprinkled in "live" project work to familiarize students with real-world problems. For example, in a VLSI design program, one of the courses required teams of three to four students to design an actual chip. In mechanical engineering, students were designing novel versions of green transportation, drawing from the likes of the Segway, the Indian auto-rickshaw, and the Thai tuk-tuk.

We built six centers in our first year. Each housed 500 students, aligned specifically with one of our sponsors. The campuses were geographically dispersed – expanding far beyond Bangalore, which was already bursting at the seams. IBM's center was in Kolkata, Tata Motors in Thane, Cadence and Autodesk in Indore, Texas Instruments in Jodhpur, and Intel in Bolpur.

One of the biggest challenges of this venture was recruiting the right faculty. I tried to address this up front by launching the venture under the MIT brand, which certainly helped. But the salaries, which were competitive to those at MNCs, also played a major role in recruiting talented engineers who were passionate about teaching.

We tried to work with Infosys, Wipro, and the Indian majors as well, but we quickly learnt that they had the classic NIH (not-invented-here) syndrome. Banking on the idea that their training capabilities were as solid as ours, they clearly underestimated the quality of our faculty and the power of following closely the MIT curriculum. For our part, we initially segmented our target market to the multinationals, focusing on companies like TI, IBM, Accenture, Cadence, Autodesk, Intel, Microsoft, and thus, setting aside Indian companies unless they contacted us. By 2015, however, they were all working with us.

As batches of students finished our two-year intensive program, we renewed our contracts with sponsors, recruited new sponsors, and opened new centers all over India. These contracts were extremely lucrative for us – we charged Rs. 6 lakhs ($12,000) per student at Rs. 1 lakh ($2,000) per trimester. We operated in a technology-enabled services business model where sponsors could simply log into our Web site and request how many students they needed each year. It allowed us to finance great infrastructure, afford and attract quality faculty, and address the engineering education crisis that India was facing.

Among our many opening decisions we made a few key strategic choices making it possible for us to build the $3 billion–a-year company we have today. First, we framed the engineering education problem as a corporate problem where more talent was essential, and we asked that they pay for a quality solution. They did. Second, we did not allow compensation to be a deterrent for hiring talented faculty. To the contrary, those with a passion for teaching could happily choose an academic career. Finally, we chose the

MIT brand umbrella, gaining instant credibility among sponsors, faculty, and students.

In 2020, an MIT India center in Indore or Jamshedpur is a thriving, colorful campus where cutting-edge innovation in science and engineering is hotly discussed. Students stream in and out of labs, dreaming of a new material to advance the semiconductor industry, or a new drug to wipe Alzheimer's from the face of the earth.

Perhaps our greatest accomplishment has been to inculcate MIT's ethos of curiosity and innovation into the minds and hearts of our graduates, creating one of the most powerful engineering workforces in the world. And one that can not only build, but can also invent.

LUCID

In 2004, my husband Dominique Trempont and I started investigating the issue of K–12 education, especially in math and the sciences. Our shared interest in education and our increasing awareness of the decline in the number of American kids pursing science and technology careers was a core impetus.

Dominique had been Steve Jobs's right-hand executive in turning around NeXT Computer and selling it to Apple, paving Steve's return to his alma mater. He had also been CEO of Gemplus, a world leader in smartcards, and Kanisa, a knowledge-management software company focused on automating customer service. His experience with education, however, came from being on the board of the International School of the Peninsula for five years.

As part of this endeavor, we did macro-level market research and interviewed a number of teachers and parents at various high schools throughout the Bay Area, deriving direct, experiential feedback from the field. We asked questions about class sizes, skill-gap analysis, teaching methodologies, and supplemental tutoring. At San Francisco's Galileo High School, Chris Kaegi, a young, bright math teacher, shared a particularly important perspective: "I have a general sense of my students' skill gaps, but I have 180 students, so even if I know the weak areas, I can't do anything about it."

Two core nuggets came out of these interviews: (1) there was no standardized methodology of teaching; and (2) there was no methodology for personalized skill-gap analysis.

Without such methodology, a growing chain of problems arose as a child moved from one grade to the next. A C in seventh grade algebra degraded to a D in eighth grade, followed by an F in ninth grade. If you don't know how to do fractions, how do you solve quadratic equations?

Lucid was founded upon these foundational blocks, which held implications far beyond local schools and students.

Another scary issue also rose to the forefront. "With an average annual salary of only about $43,000, teaching does not compare favorably with other professional opportunities available to talented individuals," a 2002 National Education Association research study reported. Less than a third of the teachers and tutors teaching math and sciences had relevant backgrounds. And American schools expected these teachers to come up with the teaching methodology, then execute on it. As if every teacher of algebra or arithmetic was expected to reinvent the wheel!

In India, however, a very large number of students were graduating with advanced degrees in math and sciences, and we saw an opportunity to apply this talent pool to a scalable technology-based teaching methodology that all teachers, all over the world, could use.

First things first: artificial intelligence. I had founded two companies based upon AI principles, and Dominique ran Kanisa, which was based upon the fundamental concept of a knowledge base (a special kind of database for knowledge management, providing the means for the computerized collection, organization, and retrieval of knowledge). With this deep knowledge of AI, we concluded that we needed to align a knowledge base of content with a methodology of teaching. This methodology would include personalized skill-gap analysis, such that a student studying basic algebra could be tested to identify exactly where his or her knowledge gap was.

Be it in dealing with fractions or exponents, this knowledge base and analytics software was capable of getting to the heart of the problem.

Furthermore, one of the key findings of our research was that children have different styles of learning. Based on the writings of Howard Gardner, a developmental psychologist from Harvard, we studied the theory of multiple intelligence – kinesthetic, interpersonal, verbal-linguistic, logical-mathematical, naturalistic, intrapersonal, visual-spatial, and musical. Our assessment systems categorized children based on their style of learning, directing them down the right track, such that once their skill gaps were identified, they were taken through the remedial track best aligned with their learning style. A kid with a visual learning style, for example, could be taught fractions in visual diagrams, while a musical child would gain access through musical analogies.

Of course, venture capitalists were none too fond of the education market, since many – including the legendary John Doerr – had tried to penetrate it with only marginal success. Those who did march bravely into the market often languished in an under-capitalized never-never land, unable to take on big problems due to insufficient funding. And so, conventional wisdom followed that you don't make money in education.

However, in 2008, the Web 2.0 era was fully manifest, and we met Edward Fields, founder of the education venture HotChalk, a free online community application that aimed to connect teachers, students, and parents from kindergarten through grade 12. Unlike many other efforts, HotChalk seemed to be getting real traction.

The brilliance of HotChalk's strategy? The company didn't even try to sell to school administrators. They were tapping the core users: teachers, students, and parents. HotChalk was launched in September 2004, and membership had climbed to more than 375,000 teachers by early 2008. More than 7.1 million monthly unique visitors from 188 countries were also using the site. That touched 72,000 schools, 93% of which were in the US.

Against this backdrop, in 2009, we founded Lucid with $8 million in Series A venture capital led by Emergence Capital. It was a PowerPoint financing, with no other asset yet in place. It took us three years of absolute stealth-mode research and development to come up with a scalable methodology for math (arithmetic, algebra, geometry, trigonometry, and calculus) to cover grades 6–12. We then created and licensed an enormous amount of content aligned with the methodology at our development center in India. We involved teachers who had particularly stellar reputations, studied their "art" in great depth, and encapsulated as much as we could into a "science."

Then came the go-to-market challenge.

Our target market was teachers, students, and parents. In 2008, there were 3.2 million teachers, 55 million students, and over 140,000 public and private schools in the US. Globally, there were 29 million teachers and 464 million students. The English-speaking international market alone included an additional 1.3 million teachers. Beyond that waited the non-English-speaking world, encompassing China, Latin America, the Arab countries, and Europe. The one thing in common: a lack of essential educational resources.

While we wanted this to be a worldwide service that every math teacher at every school in every country adopted to teach every single one of their students, we had to segment the market and find a business model that allowed us to penetrate and get early traction.

We chose North America, partnering with HotChalk. Together, we created a community for middle school and high school math teachers to interact, exchange ideas, and organically engage one another. We also developed a collaborative community of middle school and high school parents at each of the schools our teachers taught in. Most importantly, every teacher who adopted our methodology in their school managed to get the buy-in of the parents to pay for the service. This was very important from a business model perspective since it allowed us to bypass the school systems altogether. However, it also meant that our target customer base remained constrained to affluent families in North America. We did have teachers and families using our service elsewhere in the world, including India, the UK, the Middle East, and Australia, largely due to word of mouth, but by and large, we consciously chose not to fight the battle yet of tackling the less affluent segments of our eventual target audience.

We accepted this segmentation reality for five years, which allowed us to refine our methodology, build company valuation, raise a great deal more financing, and expand into other subjects, including biology, physics, chemistry, world history, world geography, English, and English as a second language.

All the while, we grew our revenues at an average 113% CAGR.

We could have become profitable by 2017, but we took our time. We were addressing a big problem, and we chose to do it right. It involved getting a high degree of personalization in our methodology and the right content to support that level of personalization. The personalization ranged from learning styles to skill-gap analysis to interest-based examples. To a soccer fan, for example, Lucid explained concepts of physics like velocity and acceleration by using metaphors from the field. We also invested in building highly influential content partnerships with the Discovery Channel, A&E, CNN, and Netflix where their content was seamlessly integrated into the flow of our history, art history, geography, and other courses.

We became so well known as an effective K–12 teaching methodology by 2018 that the Gates Foundation came to us with a proposal to fund a rollout of our methodology into poorer schools the world over, providing the missing piece of our intended puzzle.

And that is where we stand today – operating margin of 29% against revenue of $5.6 billion – a world leader in educational technology.

MAYA RAY

One of the key issues that India was wrestling with in 2008 was how to preserve the country's integral outsourcing industry, which remained largely entrenched in the major metro areas: Delhi, Mumbai, Bangalore, Chennai, Hyderabad, Pune, and Kolkata.

The urban cost structure was rising in all dimensions from real estate to wages, competition for talent was severe, and attrition rates were high. The workforce was highly unstable. Companies who invested in training employees would often lose them as they callously jumped ship without a moment's notice. Rural and small-town India, in contrast, seemed attractive both cost-wise and culturally, offering more loyalty and stability, as well as better return on investment for quality training. In the face of rising costs and complexity, everyone agreed that rural and small-town BPO was an essential strategy for maintaining the labor arbitrage advantage.

Another opportunity we zeroed in on was not on the Indian side, but the American. While the Indian BPO industry was primarily servicing larger companies in the US, another five million small businesses with significant outsourcing potential dotted the landscape. Even if such businesses only outsourced a modest $5,000 per year, this segment would top $25 billion.

Of these small businesses, one segment was particularly interesting: doctors' offices. At the time there were more than a million physicians in the US, including family and general practitioners, surgeons, pediatricians, dentists, psychiatrists, chiropractors – the list goes on. A large percentage of these were in small private offices, which, by their very nature, had significant insurance claims processing needs, as well as the standard billing, payroll, collections, accounting, and tax-related needs. Doctors were effectively running full-fledged small businesses. And collectively these small businesses made up a multi-billion-dollar business opportunity if we could crack the formula for customer acquisition in this utterly fragmented market. This was the investment thesis behind our BPO venture, Maya Ray.

To begin, we launched the Maya Ray brand through a sharply targeted advertising campaign on Epocrates. Epocrates provided clinical reference content to healthcare professionals on their handhelds, PDAs, and smartphones. With the content, they also delivered advertising. More than 500,000 healthcare professionals, including more than one in four US physicians, actively used Epocrates's mobile and Web-based content services. It was the perfect vehicle for Maya Ray, our ultimate medical office assistant.

Twelve years later, Maya Ray boasts 90,000 small doctors' offices as clients. For most, we deliver a comprehensive set of services, from secretarial to claims processing to billing, collections, accounting, and taxes. On average, each client pays $1,000 per month, amounting to $12,000 annually.

In 2020, our annual revenue stands at over $1 billion.

On the service delivery side, of course, we started with the notion of rural and small-town BPO. We took gradual risks in selecting our locations and did not go straight to a remote rural destination. Our first major back-office operation was in Howrah, near Kolkata. It had a large population and no other BPO employer, making it easy to recruit and retain talent. At the same time, it was close to Kolkata, a major metro, which gave us access to experienced management talent.

Slowly, we built successful operations in Barakpur, Krishnanagar, Uttarpara, Ulubaria, Midnapur, Haldia, Bolpur, Madhyamgram, Barasat, Naihati, Chandennagar, Sreerampur, Uluberia, Murshidabad, Bandel, Purulia, Chittaranjan, Bardhaman, Bankura, Durgapur, Asansol, Malda, Raiganj, Siliguri, and Jalpaiguri – all small towns in West Bengal. On the positive side, these heavily rooted agriculture and manufacturing regions had no other BPO employers, so our entry into these markets created tremendous enthusiasm. On the other hand, none of these towns supplied any trained management talent either. To overcome this, we recruited designated general managers from each location and trained them extensively at the Howrah operation. Then, embellished with a tray of perks, we moved them back to their hometowns. These perks included cars, chauffeurs, houses, maids, cooks – a positively luxurious lifestyle – for which, in exchange, we asked for their loyalty, commitment, and hard work.

I was once invited to the home of one of our general managers in Purulia. She was a mid-thirties woman, formerly an employee of TCS Kolkata. Originally from Purulia, she had reached a point in her life where she wanted to move back. Maya Ray had given her that opportunity, returning her not to her childhood home, but to a sprawling two-acre property, where she lived with her husband, three children, in-laws, and household staff. Her husband's two brothers and their families also lived in the homestead as an extended family. A beautiful papaya orchard surrounded the main house. And at dinner they served a wide variety of vegetable dishes all grown on the property, as well as fish from their pond. As we sat eating, talking into the dusk, there was no question in my mind that her lifestyle was more luxurious than mine in Menlo Park. But here, in India, such things were economically viable – they were, in the end, sound business.

Each of our operations employed 5,000 people, and by 2015, we had 25 operations in the small towns of West Bengal, with a total workforce breaching 125,000 people. We started with an average Rs. 10,000 ($200) per month salary, although that rose to Rs. 20,000 ($400) over the next 10 years.

During the past five years, we have used 10 of the small-town operations as hubs to create rural centers. Each small-town center manages 10 rural centers of 100 people each. This experiment was important for us as we were also deeply committed to making the development-economics angle sustainable and widespread. India's development, without question, had to include a comprehensive strategy for bringing rural India out of its underleveraged state.

We were perfectly aware of the challenges of bringing up these rural centers. English was not widely spoken, infrastructure was even weaker, office buildings were of inadequate quality, and broadband was unreliable. But the low real estate cost and various other advantages compensated for these drawbacks.

Training was also a challenge, but not insurmountable. We created a PR campaign focusing on the lifestyles of our rural and small-town employees to attract trained managers away from the chaos of big cities, traffic, small apartments, and pollution. And what our employees lacked in terms of language or computer skills, they more than compensated for in work ethic, commitment, and desire to learn.

I still remember a young man who came to interview during the early days of the Bankura operation. In 102-degree heat, he had cycled in what looked like a newly purchased black suit. He was drenched in sweat, embarrassed and helpless. But past the lack of sophistication, I saw in that moment both innocence and work ethic that, to this day, sustains the company's culture. These are not the kind of people who jump from company to company three times a year. They are the kind upon whose shoulders and hearts companies can be built to last.

The basic attitude and intelligence level was also excellent, and since my philosophy has always been, "Hire for attitude, train for skill," we knew from the get-go that training was something we would invest heavily in. They worked 12-hour days without a frown and celebrated Holi, Durga Puja, and Saraswati Puja with their colleagues and families on the office grounds.

On the operational side, we also made some important decisions so as to be able to both scale efficiently and gain access to customer bases through partnerships. We derive efficiency by using software-as-a-service vendor partnerships with AthenaHealth, Intuit, and others who provide enabling technology, as well as referral business. In many cases, they resell our services as part of their own portfolio, or they simply treat us as an extension of their own service offering.

In 2020, thus, Maya Ray's workforce spans the length and breadth of West Bengal. Other such ventures have blossomed throughout India, following our example. One, based in Madhya Pradesh, focuses on back-office work for an equally large segment: US law offices. Another, based in Rajasthan, works for the hospitality segment. Overall, the rural and small-town BPO sector now employs two million people, generating close to $10 billion in revenues. Not from the city centers – not from Kolkata or Delhi – but from lesser-known and now booming rural outposts. Here India has expanded its core competencies and, in doing so, broadened the mighty tiger's play on the world's stage.

TAXONOMY

At the end of the first decade of the twenty-first century, India was riding high on outsourcing. But for all its advancements, India was yet to produce a global software company with either original technology innovation or productization. Barring a few exceptions, the glut of venture capital chasing India found it difficult to be deployed. There was way too much money and way too few deals. Instead, tech-sector VCs were diverting capital to retail, real estate, hotels, and other non-tech sectors.

Our response: Taxonomy was founded with the ambition of becoming no less than India's flagship software product company.

To determine its market focus, we looked at the largely unaddressed problem domain, unstructured data management. Within the context of business intelligence, this was an open problem that I identified as the premise for a substantial company.

The most potent competitor was Europe's second-largest software company, Autonomy. At the time of our initial research, Autonomy's numbers were impressive. Revenues were up 47% to $500 million in 2008, even as the global recession raged. Their pre-tax profit was $208.8 million, up 84% from 2007. They had 20,000-plus customers, 400-plus value-added resellers (VARs) and, 400-plus OEM companies with licenses to more than 500 products. And most importantly, the size of the problem they were addressing continued to escalate. Enterprises were facing a deluge of unstructured information, with 80% of total business data falling into this category. Gartner observed that the volume of this data was doubling every month. Most of the business intelligence market, however, was based on structured data management and manipulation technologies. So as the amount of unstructured data continued to grow, so too did the challenge for the modern enterprise in trying to understand and extract meaning from it.

I had substantial experience in the enterprise software space, having worked both with startups and large ISVs like SAP. In fact, when I worked with Nimish Mehta, an SVP at SAP in 2006, I had the opportunity to examine enterprise search from their vantage point. With this knowledge base, I minutely evaluated the opportunity to take Autonomy on with a core suite of search technologies, and I concluded that offering it to the world of developers as free, open-source building blocks would dramatically change the rules of the game.

India did not really have experienced product managers when we started, which meant we had to recruit qualified people from Silicon Valley and move them to India. The 2008 financial crisis and resulting recession proved unquestionably beneficial for us from the recruitment standpoint, as we moved hundreds of very experienced product people – managers, engineers, architects, algorithms experts – who had found themselves out of work in America. And they, in turn, groomed the next generation of talent, eager to learn, anxious to move beyond the achievements of their predecessors. In fact, many of the product managers who came to work in India were not even of Indian origin. They came, instead, towards a world-class career opportunity.

Our search technology suite encompassed various different flavors of algorithms, recognizing the long-overlooked fact that different applications needed different algorithmic and architectural underpinnings. We studied applications ranging from compliance, archiving and retrieval, product catalogs (including recommendation engines), tacit collaboration, knowledge management, customer support, and content management. The building blocks included automatic classification and taxonomy generation, clustering, natural language processing (NLP), sentiment analysis, various types of query processing and management, collaborative filtering, and speech analysis. Both architecturally and algorithmically, we achieved a world-class product suite.

We introduced these blocks to the public in 2010. A highly targeted Twitter and blog campaign generated buzz about our arrival. One such leveraging point of this campaign: open-source guru Brian Behlendorf. Brian, a member of our advisory board, tweeted about Taxonomy to his followers, and immediately, 25 of the most influential open-source bloggers ran with the thread.

Within two years, we had 3.3 million downloads by over 200,000 active users. Almost 40,000 applications were built on top of our building blocks, and we generated 500 paying customers following the classical commercial open-source business model – free basic software, with paid premium modules, as well as paid support and training. Open source allowed us to be more a marketing-oriented business than a sales-oriented business – although we retained both a substantial Indian telesales organization, as well as a direct sales force for deals above half a million dollars. In many of these deals, we competed head-on with Autonomy and won. Word was spreading in the developer community that an inexpensive yet comprehensive technology option, capable of bringing unstructured data management applications to market rapidly, had emerged in the open-source domain.

We also took advantage of our generous India operation of 3,000 people, offering services alongside our products. Often, our customers would not only buy our products, but also a development team from us. This allowed us to create a tremendous exit barrier in our customer base, which Autonomy could not compete with. It also enabled us to innovate in every project, while also learning in close cooperation with our customers what innovations would further enhance our core engines. For example, a customer in Romania working on a mobile vertical search application brought to our attention the specialized requirements of mobile interfaces, which meant we had to process more in the back end. Other key learnings were as varied as device-specific nuances and domain-specific requirements, even social media–related data structures – all of which broadened not only our competencies, but also our reach.

We grew to $30 million in 2012, $240 million in 2015, and all the way to $1.2 billion in 2020. We maintained a product-service mix of 70%:30%, ensuring us an immensely attractive P&L structure with 20% net profit. All in all, our market cap in 2020 grew to $7 billion.

Some of our OEM partners have also built very successful independent software companies. One of them, an e-commerce personalization ISV, is now doing $120 million a year in profitable revenue. Another compliance vendor is doing $76 million, catering mostly to global 2000 enterprises. A third customer, a self-service vendor, is already up to $67 million. This year, we look forward to rolling up a large chunk of the application layer developed on our platforms. Each of them already includes hundreds of our developers as part of their extended engineering organizations, so integration will be relatively smooth. But we can aggregate almost a billion dollars in additional revenue by assembling 27 of these segment-leading ISVs.

It has been a very interesting journey so far, leading the movement of productization in the Indian software industry. A fundamental industry-level cultural shift is no small task to take on. Of course, the strength India has traditionally possessed in services is something we and our compatriots leveraged extensively. But the open-source model has now been added to the mix, proving wildly beneficial and scalable for many of the companies now ramping up alongside Taxonomy.

Some 13 years ago, I wrote my highly controversial column for *Forbes* called "The Coming Death of Indian Outsourcing," taking to task the industry's captains for being complacent and lacking imagination.

Well, today in 2020, India has moved unambiguously out of that uninspired rut. A thinking, thriving Indian software industry has emerged. Products are being built. Innovation is rampant. And at the head of this renaissance, Taxonomy is striding ahead.

CONVERT

It was clear to me in 2008 that India's journey forward as a center of excellence in software would not gain legitimacy without a home-grown, on-demand software-as-a-service company that reached critical mass.

Market research firm IDC forecasted in 2009 that "the harsh economic climate will actually accelerate the growth prospects for the SaaS model as vendors position offerings as right-sized, zero-CAPEX alternatives to on-premise applications. Buyers will opt for easy-to-use subscription services which meter current use, not future capacity, and vendors and partners will look for new products and recurring revenue streams. As such, IDC has increased its SaaS growth projection for 2009 from 36% growth to 40.5% growth over 2008." IDC also predicted that by the end of 2009, 76% of US organizations will use at least one SaaS-delivered application for business use, and the percentage of US firms which plan to spend at least 25% of their IT budgets on SaaS applications will increase from 23% in 2008 to nearly 45% in 2010.

To me this also read like a forecast for how the Indian IT services industry would lose significance as their bread and butter – complex software integration projects at large enterprises – started diminishing in scope. India, I thought, needed to leverage the SaaS wave, not get washed away by it.

Convert was founded to be India's flagship SaaS company.

However, SaaS was quickly becoming an increasingly crowded space – over 500 companies saturated the sector, addressing various slivers of business functions. Enterprises and small–medium businesses were eagerly adopting these solutions, but the sheer number of vendors and fragmented services was fast approaching an unmanageable scale. Even a relatively small business had to manage 25 different SaaS applications within its sales and marketing function. There was Salesforce.com, Zoho, and NetSuite for contact management; iContact, aWeber, and ConstantContact for e-mail marketing; InsideView for opportunity intelligence; LucidEra for business intelligence; Genius for opportunity alerts; Jigsaw for business contact data; Hoovers for business information; Xactly for sales compensation; Apptus for contract management; EchoSign for contract signing; Webex, DimDim, ON24, and Citrix for webinars and online demos; and numerous other technologies for sales and marketing organizations to navigate.

On top of this, the very disciplines of sales and marketing had evolved such that online marketing, especially search engine marketing (both paid and organic), had become an incredibly powerful lead-generation mechanism essential to the workflow of any marketing strategy. This added another layer of tools and technologies, like Marin Software for paid search optimization and Enquisite for organic search engine optimization.

And guess what? This suite of tools and technologies cost a substantial amount of money, and as disjointed as they were, integration was a real hassle. Data existed in disparate systems, with no visibility from one to the next. Even when some vendors had the foresight to integrate the offerings with partner systems, the salesperson's desktop remained a mess.

Beyond this, there was also a total lack of functionality even among market leaders. iContact, for example, offered an e-mail marketing system that worked only with opt-in e-mail lists, paying no attention to the fact that such lists needed to be *built*. Productivity requirements were poorly understood as well. A salesperson who needed to e-mail 50 prospects fitting a certain sales cycle criteria continued to have to do a tremendous amount of manual work, customizing each e-mail by hand.

Every time I ramped a new consulting client's marketing and sales, I wished I had a preconfigured box of tools – a fully integrated and configured technology suite structured according to my own methodology for bringing products to market. So, in Convert, we set out to build this preconfigured methodology "box."

Together, the fragmented CRM applications made up the overall customer relationship management (CRM) market. Gartner predicted that the SaaS market would reach $8 billion in 2009, a 22% increase from 2008 revenue of $6.6 billion. And Datamonitor estimated the 2008 on-demand CRM market at $1.7 billion, forecasting it to achieve a compound annual growth rate of 17.4% from 2007 through 2013.

CRM was a relatively old industry, and experienced executives and product managers from this industry were abundant. It was easy for us to recruit both a CEO and an executive team with deep domain expertise to translate the Convert investment thesis into reality. My friend Tony Scott, a longtime executive recruiter in Silicon Valley, worked closely with me to find an excellent team with experience at Oracle, Siebel, Salesforce.com, and a host of other Valley startups. We specifically went for executives who had both large company and startup experience to ensure that we planted the right DNA to kick things off, but also guide us as we scaled.

In 2010, Convert's SaaS suite was launched. It was a culmination of generations of experiments in sales automation and customer relationship management innovation, but built within one integrated architecture and, most importantly, accessible through a very affordable pricing structure. In fact, the Convert sales and marketing methodology and associated SaaS suite was available for free until the number of contacts in the database exceeded 1,000 records. It included a wide range, from early lead generation, prospecting, SEM/SEO, e-mail marketing, to contact and opportunity management, forecasting and funnel management capabilities, built-in business intelligence, social media connectors, Web crawlers, rich media presentation environments, and all sorts of cutting-edge functionality like opportunity alerts and triggers that had just then come into play. In short, Convert was the most comprehensive suite of sales and marketing solutions on the market.

But it was not just technology; it was a methodology, emanating from the core philosophy that marketing exists to generate sales and that targeted, tightly segmented marketing, rather than spray and pray, is what generates the best results. I had already written a book called *Positioning: How to Test, Validate, and Bring Your Ideas to Market* as part of the *Entrepreneur Journeys* series in which I discussed at length my insights on strategic marketing. Convert's methodology closely followed those guiding principles.

And ours was, by design, the least expensive solution on the market. In one stop, customers could access the entire suite of tools, technologies, and data they would otherwise be forced to pursue through 25 different vendors, at 25 times the price.

We offered more than a contact management shell that depended on customers for its effectiveness to get populated. We provided a shell already stuffed with data – especially leads, that critical incentive which makes every salesperson's mouth salivate. We had also built in mechanisms to induce account managers to insert additional data to get, in return, additional leads, thereby addressing CRM's eternal complaint around sales reps' unwillingness to populate the databases.

Finally, our product design was very much Apple-esque, with a diligent focus on usability, integrating seamlessly with social media, Twitter, Facebook, LinkedIn, and others. Clicking on the name of a contact instantly opened a window with his or her social media profiles and touch points, as well as suggestions on who might be able to provide the best referral into the prospect.

By 2012, we had 4,000 customers and 30,000 users. By 2015, the number of customers went up to 32,000 and the number of users to 400,000. And in 2020, the number has reached 100,000 customers and two million users. Revenue climbed from $15 million in 2012 to $200 million in 2015, and it is forecasted to touch a billion dollars this year. And in doing so, we wiped Siebel (by then, a part of Oracle) from the face of the earth and destroyed Salesforce.com with our pricing structure. In fact, it was in Salesforce.com's customer base that we found our initial adoption. Michael Arrington at TechCrunch saw our product suite and value proposition – and our desire to take on Siebel and Salesforce.com – and wrote about us early on, saying, "Finally, the fragmented CRM space receives a thorough consolidation and democratization in the hands of Convert." Arrington, at the time, was extremely influential with a readership of 7.5 million unique visitors and 20 million page views a month, and he loved the David versus Goliath story. His coverage triggered huge PR in online media, and the following month, CIO magazine ran a feature on us. Soon, every CIO wanted to evaluate us, eyeing the sizable cost-shaving opportunity.

Yes, we converted. We converted marketing and sales aficionados around the world. And we converted thousands of our competitors' customers by offering a total cost of ownership (TCO) advantage previously unmatched in the industry. But most importantly, we converted our customers' dollar investments into volumes of quantifiable business. And for that, our customers have rewarded us handsomely.

PIA

In 2009, Web 3.0 remained unclear. I had come up with one of the most widely referenced formulas for Web 3.0 in 2007, claiming the next generation of the Web would result from combining content, commerce, community, and context with personalization and vertical search. Or, to put it in a handy phrase: Web 3.0 = (4C + P + VS).

A bit of history:

1994–2002: Web 1.0 was all about driving online commerce, with users searching for "anything" in the tangled jungle of the Web. It produced powerhouses like Yahoo!, Amazon.com, eBay, Netflix, and Blue Nile. The rush for dollars also resulted in the dot-com meltdown. Even so, people's habits around searching, buying, and selling forever changed.

2003–2007: Web 2.0 had been a relatively niche phenomenon, with hundreds and thousands of tiny companies focused primarily on social networking communities. MySpace, Facebook, and Digg were the most notable companies to emerge. But there were a plethora of others where one could "meet," "connect," and "make friends" online – habits no longer considered weird.

At the same time, we had seen a great deal of investment in vertical search companies. If you were looking for a job, you could go to a site like SimplyHired.com and search across various job portals and career sites. Or Kayak if you had travel questions. Or TheFind if you were seeking shopping advice. In each case, the sites had carefully customized search parameters (job seekers, for instance, could search on salary ranges, locations, levels, and so on). Therein lay the differentiation from Google, a generic horizontal search engine.

Finally, Web 2.0 brought an onslaught of user-generated content in the form of blogs, podcasts, comments, and reviews of restaurants, movies, stores, and hotels. Media became truly interactive, as opposed to the one-way world we were used to. Many more voices were being raised and heard. The media industry, as we traditionally knew it, had been shaken to its roots.

In 2007, however, I had felt the next wave – Web 3.0 – needed to organize itself around two different elements: context and the user. By "context," I meant the intent that brings you to the Web, your reason for surfing. Looking for a job is "context," as is planning a trip or shopping for clothes. Fundamental to context is the user. And when you fuse a specific user with genuine context, you wind up with truly personalized service.

Imagine: You are planning a trip to Rome. You are looking for a hotel around Piazza Espagna, but not something large and impersonal, which rules out the Hassler Villa Medici. You like smaller bed-and-breakfasts with charm, warmth, and character. You want an online travel agent who understands your needs and preferences, who can find you not only the right hotel but really interesting restaurants, boutiques, and shows all aligned with your taste. Normally, you use *Guide du Routard* as your travel guide, but by 2007, a gulf between travel guides and online travel-booking sites had emerged – in other words, content and commerce were fragmented. In Web 3.0, I hoped that you would finally see content and commerce come together, no longer forcing you to hop from site to site to get your job done.

Another crucial piece of the Web 3.0 evolution would require the notion of personalization layered onto user-generated content.

Some user-generated content was already becoming an integral part of travel planning at the time. At TripAdviser, for instance, travelers could report back on their experiences at hotels around the world. The missing element, however, was the notion of the individual user and his or her personal needs. You didn't want to read reviews from anyone. You wanted to read reviews by people whose taste and judgment you trusted.

In a Web 3.0 world, I was looking for a personalized travel agent to help me find and book a highly customized itinerary, leveraging all the power of previous generations of Web technology – searching (both generic and vertical), community building, content, and commerce. And beyond that travel agent, I was looking for a personalized shopping agent; a personalized career manager; a personalized car broker to find me the car of my dreams, at the right price, with the right features; a personalized matchmaker for my friend Barb; a personalized real estate agent for Monica. In short, I was looking for my personalized intelligent assistant – PIA – as the culmination of Web 3.0.

So in 2010, our new software company, PIA, built exactly that with a small team of 10 in Silicon Valley and a larger team of 1,000 in Kolkata. I handpicked the 10 in the Valley from companies like Kosmix, Rearden Commerce, SimplyHired, and Trulia, and I built a combination of four algorithms and AI experts – all computer science PhDs from Stanford or MIT – alongside three very strong product managers. In addition, I hired a stellar young social media marketing whiz who, over time, built a team of 30 in India to implement our overall marketing strategy to resounding success. Finally, I hired a talented systems architect who designed the entire PIA architecture. He was referred to me by my friend Shomit Ghose, a venture partner at Onset Ventures on Sand Hill Road, for his background in designing intelligent agents at Berkeley's human-computer interaction (HCI) lab.

Other than the HCI architect, how did I find the other eight people? Well, I had developed a standard recruitment practice in the course of my entrepreneurial career. I hired a "sourcer" – someone who takes names of companies and hiring positions, develops a list of candidates, and then approaches them to gauge interest. While I used executive recruiters for senior management hires, I always used sourcers for recruiting the middle-management, technical, and other staff positions. It was both cheaper and more effective. On this occasion, I used a long-time associate – Arlene Rudy – who delivered the seven most critical hires in PIA's history.

Our various PIA agents – who are available as free, ad-supported applications, or ad-free paid applications – were launched as iPhone and Facebook applications and used the core principles of viral social media engagement. PIA Travel, for example, had an eHarmony-like intelligent matchmaking engine to determine compatibility as traveling companions or as houseguests while visiting a certain city. If Barcelona was on your itinerary and architecture your passion, perhaps finding a compatible, English-speaking Catalonian host to show you around Gaudi's masterpieces would be the final key to unlocking all the riches of this already renowned destination.

PIA Travel had – within months – three million users, which grew to 30 million within 18 months. PIA Jobs grew to 50 million users by 2015, and 300 million users by 2020. PIA Real Estate, PIA Match, PIA Books, PIA Music, PIA Film, PIA Restaurants, PIA Dance, PIA Chef, PIA Garden, PIA Photo – you name it, we now have PIA agents for all sorts of niches, and all sorts of users, the world over.

NUCLEON

As the end of a decade approached, I felt, more than ever, that India also needed to strengthen its semiconductor industry. Indian innovators had driven such a significant portion of Silicon Valley's semiconductor movement that it seemed out of the question for India itself to be left behind.

To be fair, India was already working on chips. Large semiconductor companies like Intel, Texas Instruments, Motorola, ST Microelectronics, and Infineon had hundreds and thousands of engineers toiling at their labs in Bangalore and Noida. But they were, often, doing layout, synthesis, verification, and other time- and labor-intensive implementation tasks, while the architectures and designs were conceived elsewhere.

And so, I looked to the future in search of a product idea to put India on the semiconductor innovation map of the world. My gut instinct was to look in the domain of convergence – an area that was, at the time, going through rapid innovation. Convergence was taking place on multiple dimensions, from home entertainment to mobile phones to cars to security.

India in 2009 was seeing tremendous mobile penetration, adding 10 million subscribers a month while forecasting 450 million subscribers by the end of the year. PC penetration, in contrast, was relatively low. It was becoming clear that India's access to the global information superhighway was happening through the mobile phone. But the phones responsible for this phenomenon remained low-end.

In parallel, the West was seeing a rapid adoption of smartphones – convergence devices – with music, video, camera, Web access, even gaming console capabilities on top of the basic communication and personal data storage functions. The smartphone, for all practical purposes, was a miniaturized, hyper-integrated computer – and Apple had led the trend by putting its powerful Mac OS on the handheld, offering tremendous leverage in terms of software and user interface. The components, however, were still expensive, and to achieve this level of functionality in a convergence device such as the iPhone, the price point of the product stayed quite high by Western standards and unattainably high by Indian standards.

Yet, the applications were obvious. Indians loved Bollywood, and they loved music and music videos. Millions of people commuted on buses and trains for hours a day, a dreadfully boring experience that could easily be made more pleasurable by listening to Shreya Ghoshal or watching Ash dance around the trees with Abhishekh Bachhan. This market, without a doubt, was ready and waiting.

But they were not the only ones. Another industry seeking to reap the harvest of ingenuity on the mobile phone was banking. The banking and credit card industry in India faced enormous scaling challenges as they attempted to bring banking to the unbanked rural millions. Scaling challenges ranged from setting up retail outlets in every little town and village, to wiring up ATMs to traverse the Indian heartland. The industry would scale much faster if the smartphone was equipped with a radio frequency identification (RFID) chip, allowing the phone to function as a credit card. This phenomenon of wallet phones had already been widely adopted in Japan, with 50 million Japanese buying products directly off their phones, using the convergence device for much more than just calling and texting. If India could transition the mobile phone into a wallet phone, it would find yet another killer app.

Of course, there was a chicken-and-egg problem, as retailers needed the RFID readers to participate seamlessly in this mode of commerce. To answer this problem, I needed stakeholders from multiple industries to join hands – from the cellular handset makers, to banks and credit card companies, to a large and fragmented chain of retailers. Cellular carriers, by acting as visionaries, were in a position to significantly augment the adoption rates, delivering lasting change.

In all honesty, this was a job that Intel and Nokia were in a better position to take up. Companies like mChek and Airtel were already collaborating on mobile payment infrastructure, and Nokia had teamed up with Obopay to further push this forward at the software level. But if the smartphone became a physical credit card, it would open an immense range of possibilities – though the company that focused on building the chipset would have to accept a lower margin business structure due to the low price point of the final product, which Intel was not excited about.

That was the premise that led us to building the Nucleon chip, packing in all the sophisticated functionality of the high-end smartphones, alongside a secure payment capability and an ultra low-power design, which in itself was a huge technical challenge. Our architects took a systems view for the design and started with an architectural-level specification that took into account PCB, package, and component-level design. Each offered the narrowest opportunities to impact the overall power budget for Nucleon. However, it also required agreement from our handset vendor customers – Nokia in particular – to be able to make those design decisions. Nucleon designers clashed with Nokia's architects on issues such as multi-chip packaging and non-critical path optimizations for yield. Every architect on their side had a big ego, and at one stage, the design discussions simply became ego battles. But those battles were worth fighting. The total impact was significant, with power reductions of more than 50%.

The most important guiding principle of Nucleon was that its entire engineering miracle had to be achieved within an unprecedented cost equation, even after assuming a set of subsidies from banks and carriers. Our challenge was to do far more by doing far less.

Well, we took that challenge. Our architects went through a grueling 12-month design cycle, interacting with every EDA vendor and foundry on the planet to see what they could offer in terms of cost-saving techniques in design and process. An obvious one was built-in self-test (BIST), a practice of putting testers on chips, which significantly reduced the follow-on testing time and cost. But we really had to squint hard to find hundreds of such cost-squeezing mechanisms. It exhausts me just thinking about the sheer number of papers our team read and conferences they attended.

When we started on this journey, neither Intel nor Nokia believed we would pull it off. We approached 27 VCs, who all turned us down, citing the obvious reasons: too ambitious, too much risk, too capital intensive.

Eventually, we came up with a nifty tactic. Instead of approaching Intel and Nokia's venture capital arms, we went to their marketing. We explained that if they invested in our project, it could become a huge PR opportunity for them, internationally. Furthermore, we argued, $33 million between them over three rounds was not that much money. In fact, if they invested and partnered with us, we could get VCs to cough up as well. To Nokia, I even proposed an "album" of 500 Bollywood super hit songs built into the phone which would make rural India salivate.

To our surprise and delight, one sultry August in 2010, the Nokia marketing people started getting it. They found our ideas for the handset go-to-market strategy compelling and the wallet phone possibilities exciting. It was they who then convinced their own venture capital arm, as well as Intel's.

Of course, there was the technical challenge of what we were embarking upon. There, we tackled the objections by recruiting as chief architect one of the key architects of Intel who was doing due diligence on us. An Indian by birth, she was so excited by the idea that she told the VCs she would join Nucleon, move back to India, and help make it happen.

We also had financing from several major banks, all quite active in the Indian retail banking market. Their interest: to bring banking to the masses.

They had, at some level, probably all bargained for a write-off of their investment, but they were eventually moved by the sheer force of our conviction. Every time they sent a no in our direction, we caught it and threw it back with an ingenious "but what if?" Eventually, they could no longer slow us down. And in 2012, after 24 months, we finally had a chip that met the price-performance targets we had set for ourselves.

In 2013, Nokia brought to market the first set of convergence devices based on the Nucleon chip. The chip was problem-free, but the handset had a battery problem. We held our breath, expecting at any moment to be made a scapegoat. But Nokia showed integrity, recalled the product, and never dismissed us.

A year later, the re-launched device blew through all of their most optimistic forecasts, gaining tremendous adoption not only in urban India, but also in rural India, where entertainment was less readily available. Nokia marketed the phone with a 5,000-song collection of Bollywood super hits pre-loaded into the device. This was the idea with which we first caught their attention.

After Nokia's success with Nucleon, we were unstoppable. We had what seemed to be a bottomless patent portfolio protecting our engineering feat, making it near impossible to design around and achieve the same set of results. Thus, we were the only company with a chip at this price point, with this level of functionality and performance. The low-power technology alone was protected by a portfolio of 15 patents.

Not surprisingly, by 2014, we had Samsung, LG, and Motorola selling handsets based on Nucleon. In fact, by 2016, Nucleon had picked up 15% of the Indian handset market before growing to a mind-boggling 35% by 2020. In addition, each handset vendor also marketed complementary versions of their products, including receiver/reader technology for the RFID.

Three times in the last two years, Nucleon's management team has been invited to dine with the CEO of Intel. Each time, acquisition is the topic of discussion. Each time, we enjoy a lavish meal and politely convey our joy at having them as a major shareholder, but our even greater joy at being independent. We remain a relatively small team of 350-odd people – nimble and ecstatically working in the culture of excellence we've created.

TRUECFO

In 2008, as I worked on the *Entrepreneur Journeys* project, I started tracking several important trends. Among them was the software-as-a-service trend, which carried tremendous momentum. At the same time, I started hearing certain rumblings – "SaaS is dead," they said. "It's time for SES."

Inch by inch, certain parts of the market were moving away from software-as-a-service, towards software-enabled service. Rather than just the development, management, and hosting of a specific software application, the end value proposition was the complete outsourcing of a business process. In other words, SES could also be framed as SaaS-enabled BPO. Here I spotted India's opportunity to turn the business software industry on its heels.

For *Entrepreneur Journeys*, I had interviewed numerous SaaS CEOs, as well as a few whom I had a chance to brainstorm with about the SES trend. Jonathan Bush, CEO of AthenaHealth, was one of the strongest proponents of SES. Sabrix's CEO Steve Adams, in his quiet, thoughtful way, also pointed out that his customers were asking for BPO, not SaaS. These two interviews had resonated with me and confirmed my own instinct that something in the software market had begun to change.

In addition, I did several in-depth interviews with Jim Heeger (CEO of PayCycle), Rene Lacerte (founder of PayCycle; CEO of Bill.com), and wrote blog pieces on Everest, Intaact, and other financially oriented SaaS companies. Based on what I learnt from these discussions, and further research on the category, I decided to zero in on the CFO's office, as well as the finance, accounting, tax, payroll, and regulatory filing functions within it, as our core emphasis in building an SES business.

Soon after, PayCycle was acquired by Intuit for $170 million, freeing Jim Heeger from his executive duties. I invited him to be an advisor to the company, and under Jim's guidance we identified the 25 million small businesses in the US as our target market. This included the 20 million mom-and-pops, as well as the five million businesses with less than 20 employees. Jim and Rene had narrowed PayCycle into this segment, and they knew its behavior intimately.

At an idealistic level, I also felt that with the US economy shedding jobs by the thousands every day, a large number of people would be forced into entrepreneurship. As a lifelong believer in small business and entrepreneurship, I was writing column after column to promote entrepreneurship as a weapon of mass reconstruction. Across radio, television, and podcasts, I kept reinforcing the same message over and over again: Create your own job. Take control of your destiny.

We began by studying the existing software landscape. Intuit dominated the small business accounting software space with QuickBooks. Then there were players like NetSuite, Intaact, and Everest in SaaS for accounting. There were ADP, Paychex, and PayCycle in Payroll. In taxes, the most compelling player was Sabrix, although it had a largely enterprise-oriented offering. Bill.com was building a solution for accounts payable and receivable. For each of their products we did an intense competitive analysis and outlined an integrated suite of on-demand software, poaching the best of each genre. Our goal was to re-create the entire suite of software that a CFO's office would need to run their business, including pieces typically outsourced to consultants. Then deliver it all in one.

For seed funding, I went to a dozen SaaS CEOs I knew well. They all saw the opportunity and came through with $50,000 each. And for the first round of venture funding, I sat down with Ashish Gupta of Helion Capital. Ashish was one of the few VCs operating in India with a true product background. We had interacted many times over the years on the bottlenecks of the Indian entrepreneurship ecosystem, but TrueCFO was our first deal together. The fact that at the heart of this SES venture was a software product was not lost on either of us.

For Series B, we decided to bring in a service-oriented VC. By then, the product was getting ready to be rolled out, and the BPO delivery portion was the key challenge. Subrata Mitra, one of the cofounders of Erasmic Fund, which morphed into Accel India later, was also someone I had interacted with for a few years. TrueCFO was our first opportunity to join hands on a deal.

Not unlike CRM, the finance and ERP function had also seen a serious amount of software development by 2009. From Oracle Financial to Quicken, both Silicon Valley and Bangalore were full of developers with relevant domain expertise. We built a small, 50-person engineering and product marketing operation in Bangalore, even though I had sworn never to locate a company in that city due to its horrendous attrition culture. But the caliber of people we were able to attract was truly outstanding. I had announced on my blog the conception of this company, and resumes simply started flowing in. Good resumes. Great resumes. And from that pool, we handcrafted a high-end team determined to become more than what Purnendu Chatterji had once called *techno-coolies*!

With the first version of the TrueCFO product suite ready in roughly 18 months, we initially built a BPO operation with a 150-person team in Kolkata, where salaries were still reasonable. This team was trained to utilize the software, delivering all the related services to our end customers.

In the US, we partnered with the American Institute of CPA (AICPA), America's oldest and largest trade association with 350,000 members. There, we identified a set of accountants with their own small accounting firms, working primarily with small businesses. To these small accounting firms, our value proposition was that by using us as their back ends, they could profitably service a much larger number of clients than they were otherwise able to. We further differentiated our product on the basis of pricing – taking advantage of the compelling cost structure of an India-based staff. And for their investment, we not only provided each accounting firm with services, but we also became a source of leads in their particular geography. In other words, our online marketing efforts, through search engines and social media, generated leads from end-user clients, which we passed on to our accounting firm clients to service.

By 2012, the model was working. Across 50 US cities, we had an average of 10 accounting firms, each supporting their clients entirely on our software, using our service personnel. We were handling all financial accounting functions, including payables and receivables, taxes, payroll, and all regulatory filings. We had a total of 500 accounting firm partners, supporting an average of 50–250 clients each. In many cases, these were solo CPAs, or two to five CPA firms. Working with us enabled them to become significantly larger businesses than they ever would have been on their own.

Each accounting firm used one of our back-office reps to support 10 clients on an ongoing basis. The cost structure was such that the end clients were charged an average of $1,000 a year for our outsourced CFO's offerings. We shared the $1,000 65:35 with our accounting firms, taking 65% of the proceeds while offering them 35% as well as extensive lead generation through paid and organic search marketing efforts.

In 2013, we started implementing an additional component of our vision. We created a rural micro-franchise to support the back-end service operation. Our intent was to get entrepreneurs to infiltrate the Indian heartland, play leadership roles, and learn to run businesses, all while operating within a well-understood framework, free of wild experimentation. To this end, we partnered with SKS Microfinance to create $25,000 loans for entrepreneurs determined to set up their own operation in a village or small town. This money facilitated the initial 10-person operation, which was given a seed client – an accounting firm with at least 50 clients – to get started.

These operations, over a three-year period, grew to 100-person operations. Some, over a five-year period, scaled to 250, and a few climbed upwards of 500 people or more.

Of course, recruiting thousands of entrepreneurs who would become conscientious, and at the same time competent, franchisees was a significant challenge. It was not easy to tell just by interviewing whether franchisees would be able to execute, and we ran the risk of client wrath if they didn't. We developed a recruitment campaign in partnership with NIIT, where their small-town teachers would nominate a franchisee plus 10 employees from among their students. Beyond this, they also helped us scale the operations, in the process placing further students with the local TrueCFO franchise. For these hundreds of students, finding employment within five miles of their remote homes had not previously been part of even their wildest dreams. But now our dreams, as well as theirs, spread throughout India like wildfire.

By 2020, we have established 5,000 such operations, employing over 250,000 people. We work with over 50,000 accounting practices in the US, and we service over 2.5 million small American businesses. Our revenue just crossed a billion, and we're one of the biggest brands in accounting services in the United States. But, really, we're an Indian company. Spread well into the depths of India, you will find TrueCFOs working in the towns and villages of Sikkim, Nagaland, Manipur, Bihar, Orissa, Uttaranchal, and Meghalaya.

NIIT, once upon a time, created an educational franchise that trained people for computer-based jobs; TrueCFO, many years later, has created the actual jobs.

EQUITY DISPATCH

From the outset of the 2008 financial crisis, the airwaves and newsrooms fell into chaos, each shouting out where the collapse had come from, how warning signs had been ignored, and how to prevent such future fiascos. Even at its end, there remained endless chatter and speculation, no one without opinion – including me. So, during that post-mortem period I began writing on my blog about what Capitalism 2.0 should look like.

As my readers and I discussed the various issues, from the need for better regulation to Wall Street compensation, one particular topic took on a life of its own: should short selling be banned? By allowing short selling, was the SEC allowing value destroyers to wreak havoc on value creators, the entrepreneurs trying to build and sustain enterprises?

Many readers defended the short sellers, citing them as the best analysts in the industry – always able to detect disproportions in a stock, whether there are problems with strategy or execution in a company. My response was that such responsibilities should fall to independent analysts, not short sellers who have an incentive to tank the stock. But to this my readers responded that the best analysts become traders.

I decided to prove them wrong.

We started Equity Dispatch, an equity research firm, with an extensive India-based analyst team, focused on catering to finance professionals all over the world. On our team of analysts in India, we looked for a combination of people with backgrounds in business, finance, technology, and economics, enabling us to assess both micro and macro factors in great depth. For example, in technology, our analysts were capable of tracing macro trends like SaaS, SES, Web 3.0, and convergence devices. Then we forecast their ramifications on the players in each ecosystem, including those likely to enter a sector as certain trends evolved. We also had economic policy analysts who traced the repercussions of major moves by governments such as China, the US, and India in particular. All three economies had, needless to say, begun driving their own economic reconstruction agenda.

In setting up the business and its structure, we closely studied Bloomberg, the financial information network. Bloomberg was founded by Michael Bloomberg in 1981 with a 20% equity investment by Merrill Lynch. It provided financial software tools such as analytics and an equity-trading platform, data services, and news to the finance industry through the Bloomberg Terminal, its core money-generating product. Bloomberg also advanced a global news service including television, radio, online, and print.

We studied Bloomberg's pricing structure and spoke with a few hundred potential customers. We estimated that with a $1,000-a-month fee structure, across the world, we could recruit at least 250,000 clients for our research. Bloomberg, in contrast, catered to 175,000 clients with a monthly fee of $1,800. Our offering, however, was quite different. Whereas Bloomberg's analysis was from a purely financial and trading point of view, ours focused on value creation and company building. Ours was a laser-clear focus on strategic analysis of public companies, keeping track of all relevant innovations, startups, acquisitions, acquisition targets, new technologies, new business models, discontinuities, and execution challenges for every company within a given sector.

We looked beyond precise quarterly earnings numbers and refused to ding the stocks at the first miss. Instead, we invested the essential time to understand why a company had missed its numbers – possibilities such as investments in futuristic R&D. Synopsys, for example, required heavy investment in R&D for low-power chip design innovation. If, for that reason, they set aside $35 million and missed earnings, we would point that out as a plus, not a minus.

Under no circumstances did we encourage short-term thinking in the companies we covered, instead trying to understand their intentions to create value, anticipate trends, and make the right acquisitions to fill strategic gaps.

To avoid a conflict of interest, we avoided consulting with the companies we covered. However, through our analysis, we often provided an enormously valuable strategic framework upon which management often based their strategic underpinnings and traders, worldwide, referenced to assess each stock's outlook.

Our analysts also tracked every underhanded rumor that short sellers tried to spread, and through real analysis we systematically dismantled their false gibberish. There was no stopping the growth of our reputation. Jim Cramer, of *Mad Money*, became one of our greatest champions. Every night on CNBC, he would quote research from Equity Dispatch, pointing out subtleties that he otherwise would not have the time to unearth. Soon we were the eyes and ears of regulatory bodies all over the world, preserving the integrity of our financial markets.

In 2011, we focused purely on the technology sector, recruiting 1,000 subscribers. The annual revenue stood at $6 million. From there, we added three sectors a year, crossing the $200-million-in-annual-revenue mark in 2015. And today, we're well over a billion in revenue with 100,000 subscribers.

Throughout, we have maintained a free online media portal alongside our paid subscription portal. This section, a pure advertising play, grew to three million unique users by 2015 and crossed five million by 2020. Our CPM rates for this media property were

$25 in 2012, $50 in 2015, and $60 in 2020 – generating $35 million in 2020 revenue. More importantly, the online portal served as an extremely powerful brand-marketing vehicle for our company. Readers familiar with our insightful commentary would often transition into paid subscribers as they came to realize the truly unique perspectives of our information service.

To gain such footing in the equity market, we must have outcompeted someone. So, what distinguished us from sites like TheStreet.com or Seeking Alpha? Well, neither of those had any methodology framework. We did. Our research was consistent across all our analysts, who were trained in that specific methodology. Seeking Alpha, TheStreet.com, and other sites aggregated divergent points of view, with no real methodology and even less deep research. They were individual opinions, often knee-jerk reactions, with no consistent framework, and very often, they produced downright misleading recommendations. I knew – at one time, long ago, I had syndicated my writings to both of them!

Also, Equity Dispatch was the only truly independent research firm around since everybody else in the business was engaged in trading, consulting, and various other activities which biased and clouded their points of view. I understood this. I had worn all those hats – analyst, investor, consultant. And unbiased I was not. I did not try to be unbiased, nor did I want to be. However, with Equity Dispatch, I was certain that delivering an unbiased, methodology-based research offering with immense depth of analysis was the only way to get subscribers to pay $1,000 a month for access. For remember, I had a point to prove: the best analysis is produced through a strong framework, a good methodology – not by individual analysts, itching to trade. Itching, in fact, to dig for dirt and destroy value through short selling, rather than offering constructive guidance and holding management teams accountable for their strategic choices.

The difference, in the end, turned out to be something very simple: Equity Dispatch was about strategy, while the rest of the market saw only numbers.

INFRASTRUCTURE

GREEN VILLAGE

India's real estate development during the late twentieth century and early twenty-first century had consisted of multi-story residential and commercial buildings rising above the urban setting. In parallel, the ever-increasing flow of inhabitants from rural to urban India in search of a livelihood and a better life brought with it a near breaking point of taxis and cars, scooters, buses, rickshaws, bicycles, and pedestrians, more often at a standstill than in transit. Indian cities were bursting at the seams; getting to and from work had become a tremendous challenge. The country was advancing, but towards what?

We founded Green Village, a real estate development company with a commitment to green buildings and green lifestyles, in 2008.

Among our most fundamental assumptions was that people should work within walking or cycling distance of where they live. Whether in urban or rural settings, this basic assumption led us to design real estate from a new perspective – one that sought to unite the working and living space.

In urban settings, where land was expensive and building had to be mainly vertical, we built multi-story towers with residency spliced 75% residential, 25% commercial. We offered a wide variation of styles and size in our residential spaces to accommodate the different levels of professionals, from entry-level to executive.

In rural or small-town settings, we created carbon-free campuses dominated by sprawling pedestrian areas. The campuses, again, had both residential and commercial accommodations in multiple sizes and tiers. At eight thirty in the morning, erstwhile rush hours started looking like relaxed Sunday mornings in the park, with bicycles and cycle-rickshaws fast becoming the preferred modes of transportation on campus.

In all our projects, our architects and engineers designed around a renewable energy–based lifestyle. An aerial view of a Green Village campus, thus, showed our bustling community members moving among solar-paneled roofs over hundreds of low-rise houses. On our urban projects, these solar panels graced the rooftops of high-rise apartments, and balcony-hung solar water heater systems captured another arm of this abundant natural resource.

Among our rural customers were Maya Ray, the fast-growing rural BPO, the healthcare companies Doctor on Wire and Doctor at Hand, as well as Urja and Oishi, two artisan-focused fashion and lifestyle brands that were gaining international traction. Our urban customers included numerous IT and ITES companies, as well as financial services firms.

With HDFC we created excellent financing programs such that companies could offer some of their employees the opportunity to buy their own apartment, house, or bungalow, thereby generating loyalty for generations to come. Think about it – you don't have to drive to work, and your employer is offering to help you buy a place in the same building or campus that you work in – what better possibilities are there?

While the urban effort ramped to a few hundred projects, we increasingly focused on our rural opportunities. For the opportunity for creativity in landscaping was much greater: sprawling space, trees, lakes, fields, and orchards, and the quality of life we were able to provide was orders of magnitude better. Part of the package in some campuses were community kitchen gardens supplying fresh, organic tomatoes, cauliflower, eggplants, chilies, and myriad other seasonal attractions.

About five years into our growing history, we began collaborating with large companies like Infosys, Wipro, Tata, Reliance, IBM, GE, and TI to expand our rural campuses, housing thousands of people. Built as clusters of residential units, these campuses each had a commercial unit where residents worked. In collaboration with our new partners, both commercial and residential facilities were, needless to say, fully connected with reliable broadband service, Wi-Fi, and cable; all commercial units were equipped with telepresence systems for high-resolution video conferencing; and soon enough the campuses were also connected by Magic Carpet Roads and Lightning Rails to the urban centers.

We also paid close attention to lifestyle in these campuses, inviting retail and restaurant entrepreneurs to enhance the environment. Soon, campuses sported custom tailoring shops, ready-to-wear boutiques, and home furnishing and furniture stores. On another end, concentrations of fishmongers, grocers, and butchers amassed. The campuses also quickly developed daycare facilities, laundromats, hair and beauty salons, health clubs, meditation centers – all the necessary amenities for a healthy, balanced lifestyle. And for entertainment, the pallet included movie theaters, dance clubs, and concert halls. Soon the niche categories of service emerged as well, whereby small entrepreneurs took up all the grocery shopping for campus inhabitants, taking orders online and delivering merchandise to their clientele on a daily basis. Another crucial category of service grew around delivering fresh-cooked food, which was important because in twenty-first-century India, many of the families that lived and worked in these campuses were dual-career households.

India Today did a profile on Green Village in January 2018 where they wrote, "Green Village is in the business of building twenty-first-century corporate villages. How else do you describe the lifestyles of hundreds and thousands of people who walk to work, go home for a nap in the afternoon, videoconference with Texas in the evening, and garden with colleagues on weekends?"

By 2020, we have built a few thousand such villages, completely shifting the dynamic of India's development from a concentrated, urbanized phenomenon to one distributed and sustainable, offering a revolutionary stress-free lifestyle for our inhabitants.

LIGHTNING RAILS

Trains had snaked their way across the Indian landscape since the British established the Indian Railways in 1853. By 2008, 18 million passengers commuted by train each and every day. But train travel in India was fraught with unpredictability. The infamous story of a man arriving at Howrah station at 4:55 for the 5:00 Rajdhani Express, only to watch the train leave without him has been told far and wide. "What happened?" he asks. "Trains never leave early in India!"

"Oh," the station agent replies, "that was yesterday's Rajdhani."

But as India endeavored to join the first rank of nations, this inefficient, often lazy, and unreliable system neared the end of its days.

We founded Lightning Railways to be India's flagship venture in efficient (and green) passenger transportation. It was modeled after the Beijing–Tianjin Intercity Rail, which on August 1, 2008, linked Beijing to neighboring Tianjin at an astounding 350 kilometers per hour (217 miles per hour), covering a distance of 117 kilometers in 30 minutes. A year later, we started building the first two-track line between Mumbai and Delhi, paving the way for Lightning Railways.

Mumbai and Delhi were separated by roughly 1,165.38 kilometers (724.15 miles), but on the way, there were a number of important cities like Surat, Ahmedabad, Udaipur, Ajmer, and Jaipur, which we also wanted to connect. Mumbai to Surat was 263 kilometers; Surat to Ahmedabad another 255 kilometers; Ahmedabad to Udaipur another 252 kilometers; Udaipur to Ajmer another 274 kilometers; Ajmer to Jaipur another 131 kilometers; and finally, Jaipur to Delhi another 258 kilometers. These stops would add an extra 268 kilometers beyond a direct service, but would expand our service options to invaluable additional traffic. And the additional travel time became a moot point when put in the context of the entire journey. For during the days of the Rajdhani Express, the Mumbai–Delhi journey took nearly 18 hours, which we managed to cut to slightly over five once Lightning Railways launched in 2012.

We used the same Siemens Velaro trains as those on the Beijing–Tianjin line. The eight-car trains were similar to the Velaro E design, but 300 millimeters (11.8 inches) wider to fit a few more seats in a two-three layout. Our 200-meter (656-feet) train seated 548 passengers: 16 in deluxe class, 50 in first class, and 490 in a second class that was head and shoulders above the Indian Railways first class.

Fifteen of these trains ran along the Mumbai–Delhi segment, guaranteeing efficiency and predictability – as well as comfort. The reservation-only trains were kept extremely clean, were air-conditioned, had comfortable reclining seats, and operated out of state-of-the-art terminals separate from the long-ailing Indian Railways stations.

In 2012, we started adding track for Delhi–Kolkata, Kolkata–Mumbai, Mumbai–Hyderabad–Bangalore–Chennai, Delhi–Hyderabad, and Kolkata–Hyderabad. In each case, we followed the same philosophy of connecting important intermediate cities, adding a bit of travel time in exchange for a mass of eager customers.

By 2015, all six lines were operational, with 90 trains running up, down, and across the length and breadth of India.

Against our two main competitors, of rail and air, we lacked nothing. We competed well against air travel both on pricing and predictability, and there was simply no comparing our services with those of the Indian Railways. Their entire first-class client base, and a large chunk of business travelers in the short-haul inter-city segments, never hesitated in joining our fast-track.

Passengers waited patiently in relaxed lounges throughout India, tea in hand, knowing without a shadow of a doubt that the train would arrive and leave at the scheduled time. Unlike their past experiences of frantic mobile phone calls rescheduling missed meetings, our passengers could place their full mental energy in preparing for the content of coming meetings, not the logistics of getting there.

As in all of our infrastructure ventures, this too was an extremely expensive project. We were overhauling one of the central structures within an enormous nation. The trains alone cost $4.2 billion. The tracks added another $50 billion. But we cut the tape on the project with the Indian government offering incentives similar to the Magic Carpet Roadways venture. Then we negotiated a very substantial subsidized loan, plus moratorium, to make the economics of the business viable.

Such infrastructure projects as Eastgate, Magic Carpet Roadways, and Lightning Railways would cease to be viable without government subsidies. But the government of India had come to terms with this by the time Manmohan Singh took his oath as a second-term prime minister. And behind the scenes, Sonia Gandhi was dreaming of a modern India, a twenty-first-century India, generating policy-level movement in the parliament and cabinet to assure its arrival. By 2014, Indian politicians had become accustomed to taking bold steps towards modernization. And by 2020, India's model of entrepreneurship-based development was universally accepted as the central weapon of mass reconstruction.

MAGIC CARPET ROADS

The Confederation of Indian Industry and the Boston Consulting Group estimated that the Indian manufacturing sector would command a market capitalization of $520 billion by 2014, versus $272 billion in 2007. From cars to appliances, computers to cell phones, components to modules, India would need to manufacture relentlessly to satiate this rapidly developing consumer appetite. Yet India's road system, in 2009, was not even remotely adequate to shoulder the related growth in high-velocity transportation required to move the products from city to city, or port to port.

The road transportation ministry was making progress on a large-scale overhaul of the national highways, but interconnectivity between the national highways was still poor. Furthermore, many regional roads, which would serve as the arteries to move raw materials and products to and from factories, remained in dismal shape. I could not count the number of times I had sat in traffic jams as lorries clogged miles upon miles of road. "The bridge is broken," the driver would announce, looking at me in the rearview mirror. "Again."

In response, we formulated a project based on eight-lane toll roads, built and maintained under professional management rather than government bureaucracies, to service the requirements of the manufacturing sector. To service this glut of lorries carrying the country's, and the world's, growing demand.

The coal movement alone was huge, with Coal India sprawling across West Bengal, Bihar, Jharkhand, Madhya Pradesh, Chhattisgarh, Orissa, and Eastern Maharashtra. Beyond coal, Arcelor Mittal, Tata Steel, Essar, Jindal, Ispat, and other steel plants also peppered those states. And Jamshedpur, now in Jharkhand, was one of the largest manufacturing plants of Tata Motors. Add L&T's cement plants in West Bengal, Orissa, Chhattisgarh, and Western Maharashtra to the mix, and we were looking at a dire need for industrial capacity roadways.

Focused on traffic flow within these seven states, and among industries such as coal, steel, cement, and auto, we set out to validate our premise. First we sat down with each of the major companies doing business in the region and mapped out their transportation routes and requirements. Little gray area arose. It was clear from the onset that they needed good connectivity internally, as well as with the ports of Kolkata/Haldia in West Bengal, Paradwip in Orissa, and Vizag in Andhra Pradesh.

Our plan developed rapidly: build, between 2010 and 2015, a 1,000-kilometer network of roads connecting important nodes of the Indian manufacturing sector. With that in mind, we sketched an ever-evolving map of high-velocity Magic Carpet Roads to match the industrial traffic needs, often bypassing national and state highways, creating shorter, more direct routes.

For example, the connectivity between Jamshedpur and the Kolkata port demanded a direct link. Each month Tata Steel sent 30 to 60 tons of sheet metal to Japanese car manufacturers. But each month, 8–10 trucks would be stuck on this route, delaying the loading of ships, often missing the tide to set sail. As our roads unclogged decades of logjam, truck drivers, once accustomed to watching the sun set from behind the wheel, started discovering the joys of early nights.

We connected the Rourkela steel plants to the Paradeep port in Orissa. We connected the cluster of factories along National Highway 60 with the Haldia port. In Jharkhand, we connected NH-23 and NH-33 at several points to make the flow of minerals smoother. In Chhattisgarh, the region surrounding NH-43 called for several Magic Carpet links.

It was, needless to say, an incredibly expensive project, making financial engineering a key factor. The Transport Ministry offered 50% debt financing under a scheme called Projects of Economic Importance. The debt had a 20-year moratorium lessening the burden of financing charges. Another 25% of the investment came from the Asian Development Bank, under similar terms. Another 5% came from state governments. And the final 20% came as equity financing from Texas Pacific Group and KKR. The total investment: over $10 billion, raised in five rounds, coinciding with advancing phases of the project.

By 2015, Magic Carpet boasted a remarkable network of eight-lane toll roads, with 32 toll gates at each toll plaza to make transitions smooth and fast. Each plaza had three payment modes – human toll collectors for collecting cash or credit card payments, contactless pre-paid smartcards to be handed to the collector, and transponders for automatic passage.

That same year, we entered the project's revenue generation phase, and since our debts lay dormant through 2030, we were assured a long window to build a profitable, self-sustaining company. And build it we did. We reached the billion-dollar revenue mark by the end of 2019, with revenues growing at 70%. With such profits we began shaving some of the principal off the debt financing long before debt charges kicked in.

The network has not only had a massive impact on the cargo movement in India, it has also greatly eased the urban congestion in Kolkata, Jamshedpur, Ranchi, Kharagpur, Bhubaneswar, and beyond. By diverting cargo traffic that once clogged key access points to those cities, Magic Carpet has made way for the human flow. On average, travel time within our circuit has been cut by a third. Once hour-long journeys now take 15–20 minutes; six-hour trips, only two. The bloodlines of the great tiger are open and flowing.

EASTGATE

As the daughter of a shipping man, I grew up listening to my father's ideas on Indian shipping: the vast opportunities for container, feeder, and barge services; the need for infrastructure development at sea and river port levels; dredging and revival of once active waterways. And as I grew into adulthood and India's stature in the world economy grew – as its ships set sail for China carrying iron ore, and the US carrying clothes and textiles – so too grew the need for more robust port infrastructure to reach these ends. Gone was the manual era; today's first-world countries moved at the speed of automation.

To make such an evolution possible, one thing was very clear to me: the major Indian ports needed to be privatized and run as professional corporations, not administered by IAS officers with limited business experience. Both the financial engineering and the operational experience necessary to run a several-hundred-million-dollar-a-year corporation is substantially different from the experience typically possessed by an IAS officer. Bureaucrats by background, most of them lacked the requisite knowledge of corporate finance, especially fund-raising, to scale the businesses, and they were not the leaders required to oust the unions and mafia that had infested the ports. As a result, as businesses these ports ran at sub-optimal levels, unable to attract top talent.

I looked at the P&L of the Kolkata-Haldia port, where my father had been a board member, and saw a company that generated $200 million in revenue in 2003, and $250 million in 2006. However, the growth potential was much higher given that the macro trends all pointed to a far larger opportunity for cargo flow. Eastern India, for example, was the primary mining zone. Tens of millions of tons of cargo could flow seamlessly to and from the coal, steel, and iron ore belts in Bengal, Bihar, and Orissa. Furthermore, the Kolkata-Haldia port system also served as gateway to the landlocked nations of Nepal and Bhutan, and it maintained substantial trade with Bangladesh. For all this potential, the numbers were, at best, unambitious.

In 2010, we raised initial funding from Texas Pacific Group, an American private equity firm with experience in infrastructure projects, and privatized the Kolkata-Haldia port, renaming it Eastgate.

We needed a top-down rebuild. So soon after the financial engineering was completed, a comprehensive management overhaul swept the port. We recruited an Indian CEO with deep domain experience in the upper ranks of the Singapore Port Authority. He had risen through the ranks there as that port was overhauled through the nineties, going from a sleepy outpost to become the busiest in the world, handling over a billion shipping tonnage.

Eastgate recruited him to Kolkata, and under his able stewardship, a leadership team of executives with international shipping and port management experience was assembled from as far away as Australia and as near as Mumbai. Decisions that once took five years to make were being made with once unheard of alacrity. Extremely competent, precise, and a natural leader, this no-nonsense man plowed through reforms like a bulldozer.

The restructuring also included a significant cost-cutting exercise that included large layoffs, erstwhile impossible under an intensely unionized government-owned regime. Lazy port officials accustomed to coming to work at eleven thirty in the morning, taking tea at noon, and lunch at one o'clock, only to return home at four o'clock were shown the door. Of course, as layoffs mounted, so too did the union *dadas* with their placards and strikes. But West Bengal had changed. Strikes were no longer welcomed in this region anxious for development, for industrialization, for progress. Supported by the local government, police intervened, and even the opposition parties failed to drum up controversy anymore. The wind of change had come with gusto.

Eastgate's vision was to thoroughly dredge the eastern waterways – not just up to Kolkata, but all the way up National Waterway No-1 and National Waterway No-2. Eastgate brought under its management, through acquisitions, the fixed terminals at Haldia, Kolkata, Pakur, Farrakka, and Patna, as well as the floating terminals at Haldia, Kolkata, Diamond Harbour, Katwa, Tribeni, Baharampur, Jangipur, Bhagalpur, Semaria, Doriganj, Ballia, Ghazipur, Varanasi, Chunar, and Allahabad. A 1,620-kilometer stretch along NW-1 needed to be dredged, deepened, and rendered navigable by ships and barges. Similarly, a 891-kilometer stretch along NW-2 needed to be upgraded and maintained, along with its fixed terminal at Pandu, and floating terminals at Dhubri, Jogighopa, Tezpur, Silghat, Dibrugarh, Jamgurhi, Bogibil, Saikhowa, and Sadiya.

All this, of course, needed additional expertise and financing. Here, as technical partners, we brought in Royal Boskalis, a Dutch firm that specialized in dredging. My father had worked with them on numerous projects over the years and had maintained close contacts. For the financing, we built a coalition of Infrastructure Development Finance Company (IDFC), Citigroup, India Infrastructure Finance Company Ltd. (IIFCL), and Blackstone Group.

As our dredging team, under the guidance of Boskalis engineers, lifted hundreds of years of silt, the rivers gushed forth with renewed enthusiasm, a harbinger of what was to come.

Aside from dredging, in many cases, berths and jetties had to be constructed or reconstructed. For this, Eastgate acted as the landlord, giving out assets on a 30-year build-operate-transfer

(BOT) mode to other private parties. In Haldia, for example, 15 berths inside the lockgates and five barge jetties outside the lockgates were assigned to BOT partners.

For seamless operation, Eastgate needed jetties for bigger barges, with 300-meter jetty length and adequate backyard space for large-volume bulk cargo handling, as well as smaller barge jetties of 130–150 meter length for transloading. Furthermore, we needed oil jetties for handling tankers. We needed container terminals in the Kolkata port with heavy lift cargo handling facilities on an industry-specific basis. The modernization needs, after years of neglect, were boundless.

The Khiddirpore dock system needed to be reoriented mainly for iron ore, coal, bulk steel products, cement, fertilizer, and general cargo handling by barges of different sizes. The entire Khiddirpore dock system was linked to Bangladesh, Nepal, Bhutan, and both north and northeastern Indian traffic through rail and primarily National Waterways No-1 and National Waterways No-2. But while rail links existed, the frequency had to be increased. And road transit, once discouraged because of a serious road connectivity handicap, only became a possibility once Magic Carpet Roads solved the issue.

There was, of course, a distinct shortage of the proper equipment and technology on all fronts. Cargo handling equipment, including ship-to-shore mobile harbor cranes, had to be procured from Liebherr, a German company specializing in port equipment. Quayside container handling cranes as well as container handling equipment like reach stackers and forklifts had to be upgraded. The jetty operators made these investments, while Eastgate focused on river maintenance, lockgate operations, and pilot navigation. The port system needed new pilotage facilities, lighthouses, and satellite navigational services for both sea and river pilots. This was within the direct jurisdiction of Eastgate.

Our primary need was dredging equipment – cutter section dredgers and shallow-drafted bottom-open hopper barges were essential for transferring silt lifted by the dredgers from the river up onto the interior land-reclamation projects. These land-reclamation projects served the dual purpose of township building and, at the same time, preventing silt from being dumped at the mouth of the river only to cause siltation and additional dredging expenses.

As you can imagine, this was a massive undertaking. For five years, relentless construction, dredging, silt movement, installation of cranes, and the humming of purposeful execution boiled forth. A team inspired by the vision of a modern port à la Singapore worked tirelessly to bring to fruition the piles of sketches, the tables of architectural models, and the computers of CAD files.

All of the above was completed in phases – five dredging zones were isolated, for example. Jetties were built in groups, and terminals adopted a progressive expansion plan. But by 2015, Eastgate had a fully functioning river and seaport system that seamlessly transmitted cargo throughout eastern India. The clamor of dredging cranes dropping silt into trucks, the sight of pillars sprouting from bulldozed ground, and the dust flying everywhere finally ended. Gleaming new terminals were inaugurated with fireworks and biryani.

Almost 100 private jetty operators worked in tandem with the Eastgate port system so that cargo transportation in eastern India, Nepal, Bhutan, and Bangladesh saw significant improvement. Voyages that once took three days were now completed in one and a half.

Our revenue model came in the form of vessel-related port charges, which included both smaller size shallow-drafted ships, particularly container ships, and flat-bottomed shallow-drafted barges ranging from 20/15,000 deadweight-tons down to 2,000/1,000/500 tons for shallow-drafted riverine operations. These vessel and barge-related port charges included port dues, pilotage, lighthouse dues, and cargo-related expenses like wharfage on all cargo handled (outside of BOT contractors), which covered 90% of the port traffic. Average royalty from BOT deals amounted to 30%–32% of the cargo-related revenue earned by the BOT contractors.

In addition, the Eastgate port system owned a substantial amount of real estate. We sealed numerous deals with private parties to locate water desalination plants, tea-processing zones, shipbuilding and breaking facilities, and a variety of other projects that effectively leveraged our assets. One of the first of these deals was with Gangotri in Haldia. Later, as Darjeeling became a major tea exporter, we leased them land for a dedicated processing zone.

Total revenues scaled explosively from $250 million in 2012, to $500 million by 2015, and $1 billion by 2020. The cargo volume reached 67 million metric tons in 2012, 80 million metric tons in 2015, and 110 million metric tons in 2020. It consisted of various types of coal for steel plants, power plants, cement plants, and aluminum plants; of iron ore; of oil products; of various steel products; and other break-bulk or liquid cargo. Furthermore, Eastgate improved the traffic volume of general containerized cargo, such as steel, tea, rice, cement, textiles, engineering goods, handicrafts, and leather.

An aerial view of the Kolkata or Haldia ports today offers the image of first-world infrastructure, with their blue, white, and orange containers neatly arranged below the cranes that stand along the river's edge, their container loading and unloading zones in geometrical symmetry. That this was, a mere 10 years ago, a zone of chaotic incompetence is hard to believe.

But infrastructure and supply chain in India had been one of the most critical bottlenecks through the twentieth century and on into the twenty-first. And as with any project that hopes to rebuild a long-squared wheel, Eastgate has been a challenging effort, taking on the complexities of privatization, union breakups, bureaucratic dissolution, and the complete overhaul of technological and professional practices. But each day, as the lighthouse at Sagar Island ushers ships into the Eastgate system, it ushers in a new range of possibilities for Indian trade and commerce.

HIMALAYA SHIPPING

In the 1970s, my father launched his original liner shipping venture, Himalaya Shipping. His overactive entrepreneurial instinct had propelled him to leave the Birla family empire quite early in his career and set off on his own, albeit for turbulent waters. Through the seventies, Himalaya Shipping, started with a mere Rs. 10 lakhs ($20,000) in equity, enjoyed steady growth up to Rs. 13–14 crores ($3.5 million) in profitable revenue, until shareholder disputes tore the company apart in 1980, wiping out his decade-long effort.

By 2008, many aspects of the shipping world had changed, but in India logistics and transportation remained a clear bottleneck. But a bottleneck that I believed could be relieved with a second iteration of Himalaya Shipping. The naming of this company was purely nostalgic; the idea of ships by the names of *Nanda Devi*, *Kedarnath*, *Gauri Shankar*, and *Sri Kailash* had captured my imagination since I was a little girl. Always fascinated by faraway places, exotic destinations like Bander-Abbas, Basra, Baghdad, and Athens, which came into focus through my father's postcards, I could see these ships sailing in and out of ports in Europe and Asia, as austere and regal as the peaks they were named after. The time had come for Himalaya Shipping to reincarnate.

With the domestic market booming and the international market clamoring for certain Indian products like iron ore, India's exports and imports were up across the board. In both raw materials and finished goods, the volume of cargo had surged throughout the 2000 decade. India's thermal coal imports alone were to rise to nearly 53 million tons by 2012 – up from 40 million tons in 2009. Of this, about 34 million tons were forecasted to be consumed by the power sector, 7 million by cement, and 12 million by miscellaneous industrial buyers. The cement sector in India had been expanding rapidly due to India's construction boom. Cement production was forecasted to rise to 251 million tons by 2012, and the coal required in this production process, to a large extent, had to be imported. Furthermore, coking coal imports by steel plants was to rise to 20 million tons by 2014, up from 14 million tons in 2009.

Coal – both thermal and coking – was a clear opportunity for a major shipping venture.

Other exciting opportunities included bulk iron ore and tea exports, jute, food products, and other commodity shipments, as well as electronics and engineering goods and machinery. This was no small-scale opportunity before us.

In international shipping, there was another vulnerability that drew our attention. Danish shipping conglomerate Maersk had acquired an enormous amount of market power in the global container shipping sector by acquiring several major shipping companies, including Sea-Land in 1999 and the P&O Nedlloyd Container Line in 2005. The latter merger established Maersk as the undeniable world leader in container shipping, although it was unable to hold its 18% market share post-merger due to integration problems mainly because of internal management deadlocks across the various acquired divisions. By 2007, Maersk's market share of international shipping had dropped to about 14%. So, while the company still retained maximum market clout, its vulnerability was undeniable.

In 2010, we decided to take on Maersk with a three-pronged strategy spanning a container division, a bulk shipping division, and a barge division. And so, some 40 years after my father's maiden voyage, with his help, I launched Himalaya Shipping anew. Our first step: we searched among my father's protégés, now spread throughout the Indian shipping industry, and found Sabyasachi Hazra, then chairman of the Shipping Corporation of India, and lured him to become our CEO.

It turned out that financing for a team with such depth of experience was relatively easy. For the container division, we built a fleet of six 6000 TEU post-Panamax vessels over a six-year period. These vessels – a combination of chartered vessels and our own ships – were initiated into a global, round-the-world container service consortium featuring COSCO Shipping from China, Mitsui OSK and NYK Line from Japan, Evergreen Shipping from Taiwan, Hyundai from Korea, APL from the US, and our very own Himalaya Shipping.

The 25 consortium ships were deployed for round-the-world operations starting from New York and ending in New York, covering three clockwise and three counterclockwise routes. These routes covered Felixstowe, Rotterdam, Marseille, Port Said, Jedda in the Red Sea, Jebel Ali, Navseva, Singapore, Hong Kong, Shanghai, Tokyo, Osaka, Seattle, Los Angeles, Houston, and New Orleans before returning to New York.

Six ships named *Everest*, *Kanchenjunga*, *Annapurna*, *Nanda Devi*, *Trishul*, and *Makalu* traversed the seas under the blue and yellow Himalaya Shipping flag. Joint consortium marketing through a global network of agents enabled us to establish stable freight rates and consistent service logistics, which allowed us to effectively compete with Maersk, which was still floundering under operational challenges. From Shanghai to Marseille, the consortium agents capitalized on the confusion facing Maersk customers.

By 2012, our container business shipped its way to $36 million in annual revenue. By 2013, $72 million. And 2020, $216 million.

Not only did my father have tremendous contacts and experience, our CEO Sabyasachi Hazra brought in several key executives, each with their own specific expertise. One of them, a Maharashtrian who came to us from Essar Shipping, was keen on starting a feeder service. In 2013, we bought a fleet of six 1200 TEU and two 500 TEU feeder vessels and chartered six more 1200 TEU vessels. Five of these were deployed in the Singapore–Diamond Harbour (India)–Singapore sector, another five in the Colombo (Sri Lanka)–Diamond Harbour–Chennai (India)–Colombo sector, and four in the Jebel Ali (UAE)–Kandla (India)–Colombo sector. My father's extensive experience in running feeder services in the Middle East, Colombo, and Singapore routes, and his friend, veteran shipping man Peter Blumbach's help from Singapore ramped the business in Southeast Asia. Soon the feeder service leapt up to $257 million in revenue.

In January 2015, Himalaya Shipping also invested $12 million in ten 2,000-deadweight-ton small barges to participate in a National Thermal Power Corporation (NTPC) contract carrying thermal coal from Sagar Island at the mouth of the Bay of Bengal to Farakka jetty adjacent to the NTPC power plant site. This was an opportunistic deal since the West Bengal government literally offered up $12 million on a platter to buy the ships, as well as the NTPC contract, in order to inaugurate Eastgate's newly dredged waterways.

Each barge generated $1 million per year in revenue and cost $0.7 million to operate. Over time, our barge division grew from $10 million a year to $50 million a year as we captured market share and came to dominate the National Waterways No-1 and No-2 routes.

Besides the container and barge businesses, Himalaya Shipping also invested in four Capesize vessels of 175,000-deadweight-ton capacity, one each in 2011, 2014, 2017, and 2020, to handle bulk cargo. We joined a consortium led by Belgian shipping company Bocimar to service their 10-year contract of afreightment (COA), importing coking coal on behalf of Steel Authority of India

Limited (SAIL) from Australian ports up to Haldia. Bocimar, my father, and Sabyasachi Hazra had long-standing business ties, so the partnership was a natural. Once the cargo arrived in Haldia, it then needed to be transloaded, with the entire 175,000 metric tons of coal split into 15,000-deadweight-ton barges to go into the riverways. The Capesize vessels, *Chomolhari*, *Lhotse*, *Manaslu*, and *Kailash*, generated a revenue stream of $180 million per year from annual traffic of six million tons by 2019.

We also invested in eight Panamax vessels of 75,000 deadweight tons for carrying thermal coal for power plants like NTPC, CESC, Kolaghat, Bandel, and Sagardihi. Each ship carried about one million tons of cargo per year and generated about $30 million with $21 million in finance and operating cost. The Panamax traffic grew from four million tons in 2015 with four ships (*Dhaulagiri*, *Kedarnath*, *Sumeru*, and *Bhagirathi*) and revenue of $120 million, to eight million tons in 2020 with eight ships and revenue of $240 million.

On January 3, 2019, my father's eightieth birthday, Himalaya Shipping threw a party at the Kolkata port to celebrate what was quickly becoming one of the most impressive success stories in international shipping. Surrounded by ships, cranes, and containers, the team paid tribute to the very sources of their achievements. The entire port and all the ships were lit with candles and lanterns.

At the party, we received news that the *Lhotse* was shipwrecked off the Sydney harbor. It reminded me of 1980, when as a 10-year-old I watched my father cope with the news of the shipwreck of the *Kedarnath*. We were vacationing in Darjeeling, and immediately rushed back to Kolkata, our private life second in line to my father's business life. But on this occasion, Sabyasachi Hazra was in charge. Besides, I had also developed enough business knowledge to know that the *Lhotse* was adequately insured to protect against precisely this sort of calamity. The party proceeded uninterrupted as the operations team promptly arranged for a smooth transfer of cargo, and our legal department took care of the insurance filings.

By 2020, we added a much-needed velocity to the Indian supply chain, previously choking at every point from soil to sea. Our container division brings in $216 million in annual revenue, the feeder service $257 million, barges $50 million, and bulk $420 million. Numbers that announce a rising star in international shipping and a threat for Maersk in many markets.

GANGOTRI

In 2008, I wrote in my *Forbes* column: "Alchemy refers to a medieval science that turns metals into gold. As our planet depletes natural resources at a frantic pace, one brand of alchemy that will become critical to humanity's survival is technology that turns seawater into drinking water."

The column profiled a small San Leandro, California, company, Energy Recovery Inc. (ERI) that was at the heart of our hydro-alchemy venture, Gangotri. Dominique had joined their board right before the IPO in July 2008. As a result, through numerous meals with H. P. Michelet, the Norwegian entrepreneur behind this fascinating venture, I got to learn an enormous amount about the water industry.

ERI had created a ceramic device called the PX pressure exchanger that helped water treatment plants around the world cut desalination costs. With the help of Energy Recovery's PX device, desalination costs in 2008 had plummeted to $0.46 per cubic meter. To put that in context, ERI clients in Spain, Egypt, Africa, China, and Australia were producing over 5.2 million cubic meters of freshwater per day, saving an estimated 500 megawatts of energy, or $352 million per year in operating costs. ERI clearly had the technology to power very large-scale desalination efforts like an over 175,000-cubic-meters-per-day plant in Algeria and a 144,000-cubic-meters-per-day plant in Perth, Australia, which was delivering desalinated ocean water into the municipal water supply.

This is what needed to happen in India on a very large scale. Gangotri was envisioned to become the new source of clean water for India, a role the Ganga had ceased to play by 2010. Of course, clean water is needed in every aspect of life, from drinking and cooking, to irrigation and industrial use. So we had to carefully select what segments of the market we were going to first pursue, planning the rollout accordingly.

We studied each of these segments, assessing the pros and cons of each market. One thing that became clear was that many seaports were sitting on large chunks of un-monetized coastal real estate, where they were willing to host desalination plants. There were also significant manufacturing units around these ports, making the industrial market attractive as our market entry strategy. According to forecasts published in the *World Water Development Report* (WWDR, 2003), the volume of water consumed per year by industry would rise from 752 cubic kilometers per year in 1995 to an estimated 1,170 cubic kilometers per year by 2025. Most of this increase in industrial water use was forecasted to happen in fast-growing developing countries like India.

We did our first deal with the Haldia port in 2010, and in parallel, we also secured Haldia Petrochemicals as our first major marquee customer. HPC was close by and had ever-mounting clean water needs. Along with our initial location and customer came our first round of funding from the Asian Development Bank, who backed the first phase of the plant as a pilot, in a joint venture with Hyflux of Singapore.

While Hyflux was new to the Gangotri mix, they had been working closely on a number of projects with ERI and their CEO, G. G. Pique. The Souk Tleta SWRO desalination plant, located in northwestern Algeria, with a total capacity of 200,000 cubic meters per day, was slated to begin operation in the first half of 2010. It would provide desalinated water to the Algerian Energy Company (AEC), the state-owned national water utility of Algeria. In 2008, Hyflux also contracted ERI's PX technology for one of the largest works in China, the 100,000 cubic meters per day Tianjin desalination project.

During our pilot phase, it was fascinating to watch the speed and alacrity of Hyflux's design project. They used a lot of the blueprints from the SingSpring project designed to meet 10% of the water needs of Singapore. We used this phase to train our Indian team under the highly experienced Singapore team that had worked on SingSpring. As pipes and turbines went up, as water turned and roiled, we watched firsthand the alchemy itself – 100,000 cubic meters per day, close to the 136,380 cubic meters per day of SingSpring, for a building cost of $150 million.

Both the ERI and Hyflux names helped us establish credibility with our investors during the due diligence phase, and after bringing HPC to the table as the anchor client and successfully completing the pilot phase, we were very well situated for sustained financing and growth through extensive public-private partnerships, as well as further banking tie-ups. The same consortium of five banks – DBS, KBC Bank, ING Bank, Standard Chartered Bank, and Norddeutsche Landesbank Girozentrale – who had financed the SingSpring project were brought to the table by Hyflux.

More financing poured in in 2012 after the Haldia plant was up and running and had started servicing much of the industrial belt in West Bengal. One of our biggest collaborators turned out to be the government of Orissa. Having spent most of its post-independence history as a backwater state, Orissa was determined to find a niche, and hydro-alchemy via seawater reverse osmosis provided them with the much-needed breakthrough. Billboards along National Highway 5 proclaimed in bold, "Orissa, the New Glacier State."

By 2017, 30 Gangotri desalination plants ran along the coast of Orissa, built on land the state government provided at huge subsidy. Three million cubic meters per day of freshwater was created at a total cost of $4.5 billion. And with this Gangotri captured 78% market share in the industrial market in Orissa, Bihar, Madhya Pradesh, West Bengal, and Western Maharashtra.

By 2018, Gangotri was also feeding the utilities in many of the South Indian states through a complex grid designed to achieve maximum efficiency. The Indian government had acquired major financing from the World Bank for this smart water grid project, which IBM designed and helped implement. At the same time, we also accidentally solved a long-standing diplomatic problem. India had been planning to link the rivers flowing from the Himalayas and divert them south. However, this would cripple Bangladesh since more than 80% of its 20 million small farmers depended on these waters. But in 2018, instead of diverting large percentages of water from the Ganga and the Brahmaputra to the south, India was able to replenish the southern Indian rivers by funneling freshwater from the Orissa Gangotri plants.

Having saved Bangladesh from this calamity, we also earned the contracts for building almost 100% of the country's 1.5 million cubic meters per day desalination infrastructure in the delta, pushing our 2019 backlog up to $2.25 billion. Yes, Gangotri is a multi-billion-dollar company in 2020, but we are much more than that. We are helping solve a planet-scale problem – an enormous responsibility, but an even more enormous pleasure.

MANDAKINI

While Gangotri focused on water desalination in eastern and southern India, Mandakini utilized a very similar technological underpinning in collaborating with the Gujarat government to address the needs of western and northwestern India, as well as southern Pakistan.

Gujarat is home to one of the longest coastlines in all of India at 1,600 kilometers, a third of India's total. From the Runn of Kachchh to the northern tip of Maharashtra, this highly industrialized stretch of land houses numerous ports and the world's largest ship-breaking yard, at Alang. Furthermore, it is strategically located to address the needs of the water dispute–ridden India-Pakistan border, making it the perfect place to situate a venture positioned to function as a water diplomat.

India's domestic water distribution plan was established in 1955, when the northern states signed an interstate water agreement. According to this agreement, water from the rivers of Punjab was to be distributed to Rajasthan and Kashmir. Water to the tune of 8.0 million acre feet was allocated to Rajasthan, 7.2 million acre feet to Punjab, and 0.5 million acre feet to Kashmir. Soon after, the Rajasthan canal (today called the Indira Gandhi canal) was built to guide water from the Ravi-Beas river system in Punjab to water-starved Rajasthan.

In 1966, after the reorganization of Punjab, its 7.2 million acre feet of water was equally divided between Punjab and the newly constructed state of Haryana (each receiving 3.5 million acre feet), with 0.2 million acre feet to meet Delhi's needs. Then, in 1978 Punjab and Haryana started to link the Sutlej River in Punjab via a canal to the Yamuna River in Haryana. This link (SYL) was necessary to provide Haryana the allocated 3.5 million acre feet as the Ravi-Beas system could not meet the quota. Three years later, through much contention, Punjab, Haryana, and Rajasthan came to an agreement, allotting 4.22 million acre feet to Punjab, 3.50 million acre feet to Haryana, 8.60 million acre feet to Rajasthan, 0.20 million acre feet to Delhi, and 0.65 million acre feet to Jammu and Kashmir. As part of this accord, Punjab agreed to finish the SYL within two years. However, it failed to keep its promise, and thus disputes raged on through years of renegotiations and treaties, while the overriding water shortage went unsolved for decades.

These already tenuous negotiations were only further exacerbated when, in October 2008, Pakistan threatened nuclear war after Indian prime minister Manmohan Singh inaugurated the controversial 450-megawatt Baglihar hydroelectric project over the Chenab River, which flows from Indian-administered Kashmir into Pakistan, where it is a central irrigation artery.

Aspiring towards calmer days in this politically charged backdrop, the Gujarat government chose to partner with us on the Mandakini project. Further partners revolved around relationships built on Gangotri. First was Hyflux, the same Singapore group involved in Gangotri, and with the backing of many of the same bankers, we began breaking ground. With an investment of $4.5 billion, the first of our seawater reverse osmosis (SWRO) plants was built in 2013 in Mandvi. Its three million cubic meters per day water generation capacity was enough to support the freshwater needs of nine million people throughout the villages of Kachchh, the cities of Saurashtra, and along the river basins of the Saraswati and the Sabarmati.

In parallel, the Gujarat government negotiated several important agreements. With Rajasthan, it proposed to create a canal linking the Luni and Chambal rivers in Rajasthan with the Saraswati in Gujarat. Furthermore, it agreed to dredge and extend the Saraswati River to connect with the network of desalination plants along the coast. In turn, the Rajasthan government would create a canal system to transmit the water from Gujarat into its desert interior. Suddenly, throughout western India, dead rivers revived, gushed forth, spawning greenery and giving life.

With this tailwind behind our project, the Indian government entered a more complex negotiation with Pakistan in 2015. India offered to create a canal system, making desalinated water from Gujarat available to Pakistan. From there Pakistan would need to complete the domestic portion of the canal system in order to distribute the water to its heartland. But this would be a prohibitively expensive effort, unachievable without the participation of America. CNN announced one fine morning in March 2016 that the United States had offered to finance both canal systems in exchange for nuclear disarmament.

The Mandakini desalination plant network became one of the most vital components of the India-Pakistan peace process, attracting both international attention and financing. In the ensuing ten years, the United States invested some $22.5 billion in a historic escalation of its aid to Pakistan. Prior to this, US aid to Pakistan had been limited to the war against Al Qaeda. And most of this money was squandered by Pakistan's corrupt government, often ending up in the wrong hands, including Taliban coffers. Mandakini, to the contrary, was clearly the right hand. It would bring water to some 27 million people in southern Pakistan from three desalination plants in Mandvi, Mundra, and Kandla. It would bring agriculture, drinking water, and industrial supplies to an otherwise arid region.

Another major breakthrough in the India-Pakistan conflict was achieved around the Chenab River water. The International

Court of Justice in the Hague ruled in favor of India, allowing it to complete the Baglihar hydroelectric project, as long as India ensured that Pakistan would face no further water shortage because of it. This was primarily due to a presentation at the Hague court on India's plans to take an active role in solving Pakistan's water problems. The presentation, given by the Indian foreign minister and the US secretary of state, highlighted the role of the Mandakini water desalination project as a key strategic piece of the diplomatic puzzle. It was water diplomacy at its best.

By 2018, four three-million-cubic meters per day desalination plants were fully functional in northern Gujarat. The customers of the plants spread from the states of Gujarat and Rajasthan, to the province of Sindh in Pakistan. But the impact did not end there. In 2020, these four plants service the needs of more than 36 million people, and our multi-billion-dollar water diplomacy enterprise has become the most coveted growth stock in history.

ADISHAKTI

By 2005, the negative impact of fossil fuel–based energy was crystal clear. Dark, ominous clouds hung over the world's great metros, collecting the pollution from cars, buses, and motorcycles. Each year, fossil fuels produce 21.3 billion tons of carbon dioxide. Enough that the consistently declining proportions of greenery could not hope to absorb more than half, leaving a net increase of 10.65 billion tons of atmospheric carbon dioxide per year. Experts were fast proving the link between carbon dioxide and global warming. The Energy Information Administration estimated that in 2006 fossil fuels comprised 86% of the primary sources of energy (petroleum 36.8%, coal 26.6%, and natural gas 22.9%). Led by the United States and Western Europe, and closely followed by China, aggressive research in renewable energy was underway. Wind fields loomed over the German countryside. Nuclear power plants dotted the French landscape. Despite aggressive damming of rivers all over the world, hydropower was still not a fully harnessed source. Brazil had taken a leadership role in the development and use of biofuels. But for India, solar energy was one of the most promising.

By the end of 2007, the green movement had captured the imagination of the world. Al Gore's *An Inconvenient Truth* had left an indelible impression on consumer consciousness, sending hybrid car sales through the roof. Further momentum gathered when Gore took home both an Academy Award and a Nobel Prize for the work. And by August 2009, solar installations were cropping up across American rooftops as the *New York Times* hailed President Obama, who wanted to "make the United States the world's leading exporter of renewable energy."

To further drive the green movement, instability in oil-producing regions had long been a grave cause for concern among major energy-consuming economies like the US, as well as the emerging markets of India and China. But most importantly, the narrowing cost differential between photovoltaic electricity and grid electricity was finally making solar energy a viable alternative.

In the United States, there had been some 46 solar cell IPOs between 1995 and 2007, with 35 of these concentrated between 2005 and 2007. Total solar cell IPO capital raised since 1995 was $7.33 billion, with over 75% of that total raised between 2005 and 2007. The entire solar industry raised $5.8 billion in public capital in 2007, up from $2.2 billion in 2006, and $1.5 billion in 2005. There was little doubt: the solar sector was heating up.

India, with approximately 200 clear, sunny days a year and the potential to produce 5,000 trillion kilowatt hours of power per year, was a prime candidate to join this movement. But India's sun resource was grossly underutilized, due both to limitations in energy storage technologies and, more importantly, a total lack of policy initiatives. Germany and Spain had brought about incredible adoption rates of solar energy through feed-in tariffs (FITs). But for all of India's advances, the majority of its villages remained in a darkness unanswered by its urban governors, with the immense potential of solar energy un-leveraged.

Meanwhile, on the production side, the photovoltaic cell industry was full of relatively mature technological solutions, though not the cheapest, most scalable long-term solutions. Much of the entrepreneurship was therefore directed towards research and development of new thin-film photovoltaic cells using materials such as CIGS and organic films on different substrates, as opposed to silicon-based solutions.

Our venture, AdiShakti, was one such effort.

The scientist behind the pathbreaking thin-film photovoltaic cell was out of MIT's energy department. Backed by R&D grants from the Obama administration's stimulus funds, he nurtured the innovation in laboratories before ever exploring commercialization. He had decided early on that his market was going to be India, for all its potential. Not just in pure population numbers, but also for its cheap labor, through which he could achieve very attractive cost metrics for installation and support.

I came to this project from the other end, looking for a technology that could be paired with India's low-cost resources to achieve rapid grid parity. While Germany, because of its expensive labor force, could not achieve grid parity until 2018, India could do so momentarily. I contacted the MIT Energy Initiative through the alumni association, and was introduced to Professor Vladimir Bulovic. From there on, I asked a lot of questions, met hundreds of people, and networked my way towards the solar cell technology that became the core of AdiShakti.

Our first decision was to manufacture the thin-film solar cells in India. India had missed the entire semiconductor manufacturing opportunity, an industry that went largely to Taiwan, and then to China. We were determined not to miss the next big manufacturing sector opportunity.

Solar cell plants typically resemble semiconductor fabs, taking the wafer through a processing sequence to create working solar cells. We looked at 50 megawatt capacity per fab, spread over 50,000 square feet of plant area. The capital investment in building a solar cell plant is about $2 million per megawatt, which meant each plant would cost us $100 million in CAPEX. We ramped nine solar cell manufacturing plants from 2012 to 2018 in Rajasthan, Uttar Pradesh, Bihar, Madhya Pradesh, Haryana, Orissa, West

Bengal, Tamil Nadu, and Maharashtra. In each case, we structured debt financing for the CAPEX portion from various banks, and we raised equity from India Infrastructure Finance Company Limited (IIFCL), IFC, and ADB.

To build the plants was a herculean task in itself. Equipment manufacturers like Applied Materials were a big help, as were consultants with deep expertise in setting up semiconductor fabs in Taiwan and solar plants in Germany. The first plant, in Rajasthan, took almost a year longer than we estimated, but the team got thorough training on that project. Thereafter, the remaining plants were much more tightly managed and stayed within the budgeted time window.

Our main marketing channel in the urban geographies was construction companies and real estate developers who were riding the "green building" phenomenon. Living and working in "green buildings" had become fashionable among Indian consumers. It reminded me of the time in California when the hybrid Toyota Prius had become a status symbol. Now Indians were showing off their solar water heaters and boasting of their efforts towards zero-energy homes at dinner parties. And both residential and commercial developers were aligning themselves with this demand, retrofitting existing buildings and, of course, equipping new buildings with solar power.

The Indian government also created incentives for developers and consumers alike. Solar water heaters, for instance, came with metering technology, displaying household energy savings and qualifying consumers for healthy rebates. Developers investing in solar fitting their buildings earned significant tax incentives as well. An entire ecosystem of solar integrators developed around AdiShakti and the real estate developers. They were adept both in new building and retrofitting. And soon, soaring urban demand alone drove us to a point where, clearly, capacity was the bottleneck. That led us to building a new manufacturing plant almost every year.

We also wanted to access the rural Indian market, for which a different strategy was devised. A new genre of companies called "rural utilities" came into existence through yet another government policy incentive. Aided by attractive financing schemes, entrepreneurs started setting up decentralized rural utilities with solar farms. Driving through rural India, solar fields became as common a sight as wheat.

All over India, villagers who had never enjoyed the privileges of light, hot water, television, and numerous other modern amenities started discovering them. The delight of remote desert people in discovering an electric fan to fight the oppression of 45-degree heat was childlike. They stood around the spinning pedestals in worship. And the poorest of the poor, who made their livelihoods through carpet weaving, embroidery, basket making, and such, managed to extend their working hours till after sundown, and well into the night.

AdiShakti, needless to say, is now one of the world's largest corporations, but one built not only on a hunger for profit, but a hunger to advance. To do better. We consider it our responsibility to convert India to a 100% solar-powered economy by 2050, in the process creating enormous wealth throughout the solar ecosystem – from rural utilities to green urban builders – as entrepreneurs and government officials, each in their own capacity, advance technology and policy towards a brighter day.

RURAL AND SLUM DEVELOPMENT

FDBI

Before we could launch our numerous rural development and slum rehabilitation projects, we needed to hone our franchise and micro-franchise models to a finer edge.

Professor Raj Reddy of Carnegie Mellon University first urged me to look at micro-franchise as a vehicle for economic development in 2007. Micro-franchises are small businesses that can easily be replicated by following proven marketing and operational concepts. Micro-franchises provide entrepreneurs with small franchises requiring little start-up costs.

By 2008, microfinance had become a world-renowned phenomenon, especially after Dr. Yunus's Nobel Prize two years earlier. Borrowing small sums of money to buy cows or sewing machines had quickly become commonplace. However, micro-franchise was a relatively lesser known, but equally powerful, model. In simple terms, it is a franchise business with a centralized strategy arm that masterminds, trains, and supports the building of a large number of replica businesses. A dairy. A lobster farm. A pottery brand. Cheese. Butter. Hilsa. Soap. Fragrance. You name it.

For India, I felt, to engage much of the base of the pyramid, both rural and urban, in meaningful economic activities, this sort of central planning coupled with decentralized replication would be very effective.

In the beginning we worked exclusively with microfinance institutions (MFIs) and banks, but the more I thought about it, the need for a specialized bank for financing development-oriented projects, especially those within a franchise structure, became crystal clear. Thus, in 2012, we launched the Franchise Development Bank of India (FDBI). It had financing from the International Finance Corporation (IFC), Asian Development Bank (ADB), and ICICI Bank. IFC had been active in India for many years, and they even had a venture capital arm. They were the first investor I contacted when I came up with the FDBI project. They liked the idea and brought in ADB and ICICI as co-investors.

FDBI partnered with the top 100 MFIs in South Asia, including Grameen Bank, Bandhan, SKS Microfinance, SEWA Bank, and myriad others. When loans outgrew the expertise range of the MFIs, which was common within franchise projects, we became the handoff point.

In the early days, we spoke with hundreds of micro-franchise businesses to understand their financing issues. They confirmed the pain, but further interactions caused concerns in our own minds about their execution capabilities. Their marketing strategies were weak. The product quality was not controlled with sufficient diligence. Thereafter, instead of going broad, we decided to focus our entire business plan on a handful of strong franchises, to become the growth propeller powering each towards their ultimate scaling potential. The project – the franchise around which loans were to be disbursed – was the key to our success. Hence we identified what we believed to be the top 10 projects, and we aggressively courted them. To this end, we collaborated with projects like Camellia, Gagori, Palanquin, Deepti, Him-Icon, Urja, Oishi, Patami, Maya Ray, and Bioscope.

Patami, for example, had the potential of developing 500,000 small-scale jute-furnishing franchises across India and Bangladesh. At $5,000 per annum per franchisee, the total loan amount exceeded $2.5 billion, a large enough loan in itself to demand a certain handling, but add to that the challenge of profitably handling the 500,000 small loans it broke down into, and it became no small task.

That was just one project.

Palanquin had a different structure altogether. Their 2,000 retail stores across 300 cities, towns, and townships had to be financed, and while the number of franchisees was smaller, the loan amount was much greater. Over 10,000 units of furniture inventory had to be financed per year, along with real estate and working capital.

Another of the projects we aligned ourselves with was Maya Ray. As the rural BPO model gained success, Maya Ray and several other companies within that sector started franchising the service delivery operations. By 2020, the rural and small-town BPO sector was two million people, generating close to $10 billion in revenues. There were 100-, 200-, and 500-person operations sprouting up all over India, and it was FDBI who spearheaded the financing for many of these franchisees.

In each case, we studied the sector, the company, its business model, operational model, and financing requirements, and then we designed a technology-enabled solution best suited for that particular scenario. Where the loan sizes were small and the number of franchisees was large, we partnered with mobile phone operators to offer a contactless solution whereby the entire credit processing, accounting, interest payments, loan repayment, peer review, franchise review, and other functions could be conducted over the mobile phone terminal. The cost of the phone – often a slightly more sophisticated handset than what was common fare in rural villages – was built into the franchise. The IT system that supported the franchise was shared by the franchisor and the bank, so that both stakeholders could keep close track of the money flow, so if and when situations needed attention, both parties could intervene and offer assistance.

Where loan sizes were larger, typically, computers and Internet were available on premise. Therefore, our IT solution was designed with an Internet-banking interface in mind.

As for interest rates, we kept them around 7%. Unlike the micro of microfinance loans, ours were not $1–$5 loans. The lowest loan amount we serviced was $2,500, which meant that processing cost against capital under management was correspondingly less expensive. Besides, because we were working with only handpicked franchises, we had an excellent loan repayment rate, which inherently lowered risk.

In fact, all credit applications were jointly evaluated with the franchise applications. If the applicant passed the franchisor's evaluation criteria, the chance of their application going through the FDBI financial due diligence process was 95%. In only 5% of the cases were we finding that a potential franchisee who had already been approved by the franchisor had any red flag issues to prevent us from approving credit.

My core belief had long held that small business and entrepreneurship, not aid, was the only sustainable route to economic development. My interaction with Professor Raj Reddy had reinforced that even for rural development and slum rehabilitation, the best formula was to stimulate entrepreneurship, but above the level of microfinance ($5–50 loans). With our $2,500 minimum loan requirement, we were working with businesses that actually generated employment alongside revenue.

By 2020, the invested capital for FDBI stood at $10 billion, spanning two million borrowers from all levels of the economic spectrum. Furthermore, these franchises supported an employment base of more than 20 million people. Urban and rural.

Today the model of a core set of large-scale franchise businesses has been accepted worldwide as a rich development vehicle. Similar franchises have cropped up in China, Africa, and Latin America, and in each region, a financial institution in the image of FDBI has emerged to finance their rapid scaling. The *Economist* has done three stories on FDBI over the last decade. In the most recent, they ran a feature on franchise as a model for economic development with examples from 15 countries. "Since Dr. Yunus of Bangladesh started his Nobel Prize–winning work in microfinance in the mid-seventies, development economics has come a long way," they wrote. "Microfinance has been widely adopted, with the children of those who grew up enjoying its benefits now seeking out better opportunities. Foremost among the micro-franchise model its poster child, FDBI."

Meanwhile, FDBI and its franchise partners are quietly executing their business mission: creating jobs, creating wealth, creating tomorrow's India today.

CAMELLIA

Throughout the eighties and nineties, I watched as the Indian countryside emptied itself into the city centers at an alarming rate. Villagers came in search of jobs, prosperity, and a general uplifting from their poverty-ridden lives.

But they rarely found such conditions. Instead they found similarly small dwellings to those in the villages, but without the clean air, the incredible beauty of rural India, and the support of their communities. Gone were the bathing ponds surrounded by coconut trees. Gone were the languid afternoons with friends stretching in the village square, eating puffed rice and peanuts. Gone were the safe streets for their children to roam free.

In the urban slums, where much of the migrants ended up, the quality of life dipped to unimaginable lows. Narrow alleys winding through helter-skelter housing, through waste, through disease. Squalor. The stench of rotten fish and vegetable peels. Everyone and everything piled one upon another – it was not uncommon to find an eight-member family packed like sardines into a 100-square-foot room. But cramped as it was, it was better than the streets where gangs patrolled among wayward dogs and beggars followed passersby with blinded eyes, their grubby hands clutching at anything they could reach.

This was what the migrants found in their dreamed cities: a slum population that had gone from 27.9 million in 1981 to 61.8 million in 2001, as India's total population increased from 683 million to 1.03 billion respectively. By 2008, India was an undeniable urban disaster.

In response, I found myself looking for a model to move large numbers of slum dwellers out of the cities, back to rural India to both lessen the urban pressure and rehabilitate slum children in a healthier environment. We entered the slums of Kolkata to do our market research for Camellia, asking parents if they would allow their children to move to villages where we would house them in residential schools. The children, in turn, would study and work in a flower farm.

The overwhelming answer was that they felt comfortable letting their older children go, but not the younger ones, whom they wanted close by. That made sense to us, so we zeroed in on the 12–18 age group, which was also easier to handle as they were far more self-sufficient.

In 2008, we opened our first Camellia center in the small village of Akalpoush, near Bardhaman in West Bengal. There, we acquired two acres of land and built a large residential building with 20 dormitory-style rooms, each home to 14 students. Next came a schoolhouse with seven classrooms fully wired with broadband access. The school itself was run by Vidyangan, a sister company, while the remaining land was gradually seeded to blossom into flower farms, which our 280 students would be working.

We took our time with the building, cultivating architecture that spread itself out more as home to our students than dormitory. And as the buildings had risen bright in the sun, around them our fields began to bloom. Camellia cultivated tuberoses, marigolds, roses, lotuses, gladioli, carnations, lilies, chrysanthemums, anthuriums, gerberas, irises, and sunflowers, as well as certain ornamental orchids. In spring, our acres of flowerbeds looked like paintings, with large carpets of orange marigolds and yellow sunflower fields swaying in the gentle morning breeze.

The children played kabaddi in the open fields, happy to discover the joys of space. They studied. They gardened. They browsed the Internet for tips on how to treat mildew in roses. They came to love the smell of the soil, the feel of it in their hands, and of course the absolute joy in watching their flowers bloom.

"Looks like Kolkata, eh?" a teacher asked a group of students early in our first year. He was pointing at a purple field of gladioli, and in unison, the 13-year-olds cried, "Noooooooooooooo!"

Each morning, at four o'clock, the kids cut flowers, and then they carefully loaded our air-conditioned trucks that set out for Kolkata, bumping along the country roads, flowers spilling from their gates, where, in each of our hundred slums, a sales rep waited. "Look at these giant lilies," one of them would exclaim, unloading the pink-filled buckets, breathing in a waft of fragrant air.

We trained these reps to call on all the local venues that hosted weddings and other large-scale events. They also called on houses preparing for a funeral or naming ceremonies. Our reps had territories, and within those territories, they were to keep track of all the flower procurement needs of the community. Akalpoush was two hours away from Kolkata, and we located all of our Camellia centers within such a general radius of a major city.

Once the basic model developed, we built a franchise around it. We enabled entrepreneurs to license and run Camellia centers all over the country. From Jaipur to Patna, our franchise was in full bloom. We also enabled slum dwellers to run their sales businesses as a micro-franchise, borrowing money from one of several microfinance banks that we established partnerships with.

Soon reporters from the *Economist* to the *Wall Street Journal* were coming to cover Camellia. The *Economist* wrote, "We never thought India would be able to reverse the urbanization trend. But Camellia has changed the rules of the game." *Time* did a feature story with photographs of children working in the flower fields, contrasted with photos of those scraping a life out of the heaped Mumbai slums. Boys and girls of the same age, but no longer sharing the same future.

In 2010, we had successfully moved 5,000 slum kids to Camellia centers in rural India, mostly around Kolkata. By 2015, this number leapt to 160,000. And by 2020, half a million. On top of that, 10,000 Camellia sales reps remained in the cities, delivering flowers to anyone and everyone who wanted them. And soon, those who wanted them grew in great variation: households asked for flowers on an increasingly regular basis, and corporations, as well, soon became an integral part of our growing clientele.

Mumbai, Delhi, Kolkata, Chennai, Hyderabad, Pune, Ahmedabad, Nagpur, Kanpur, Surat, Jaipur, Lucknow, and Patna all became central markets for Camellia flowers. Across these cities, over a hundred million people lived and worked, offering us an unquenchable clientele base. In the rural hinterlands surrounding those cities, we speckled the land with 2,000 Camellia centers, raising our revenue base to Rs. 150 crores ($30 million).

But flowers were not the only source of revenue for this franchise. Camellia had penetrated 10,000 slums. We had tremendous goodwill with some 10 million slumdwellers across the length and breadth of India. Our trucks came and went unmolested through some of the most dangerous neighborhoods. And this reach did not go unnoticed by those consumer packaged goods manufacturers hungry to develop additional markets for products like soap, shampoo, and detergent. Naturally, we started developing innovative advertising partnerships.

Over 50,000 of our trucks wove through the streets sponsored by Moti soap, with a picture of Katrina Kaif holding a vase of white roses, declaring in big, bold lettering, "Moti Smells Camellia." Sunflower oil brand Suryani was on another 20,000 trucks with bright yellow fields painted in the background. Thus, in 2020, while the direct revenue of the Camellia flower franchise hovered around $30 million, we pulled in an additional $300 million in advertising revenues. A Liril deal, for example, brought us $20 million a year, while Airtel, Reliance, Videocon, HP, Nokia, and Microsoft added up to another $100 million, including some in-kind sponsorship.

How did we reach such heights so quickly? One of our major scaling factors was our ability to acquire enough land at reasonable prices. Instead of working with government middlemen in the land acquisition process, we acquired land directly. We paid fair prices, knowing that as we developed both the land and the communities, the value would grow exponentially. In fact, our 4,000 acres of current holdings acquired for about $180 million is currently valued at $2 billion. We financed the land acquisition with a debt from the IFC, and we serviced it with our advertising revenues. Gradually, as our balance sheet grew stronger, we paid off the debt with equity from the IFC and the Asian Development Bank.

Today, at our schools and in our fields, I see faces quite different from those we originally encountered in the slums of Kolkata. These faces sport healthy smiles, gentle glances, and eyes full of warmth and faith. They are neither afraid nor angry. Many of them have stayed on as part of Camellia, to teach, to staff, to help us scale additional centers. Some have even become franchisees of new centers. Others have built nurseries or become resident gardeners at places like Renaissance properties or Amrapali Spas. And still others have left for other opportunities cropping up around India, but none will soon forget the way they painted the land with roses and dahlias.

PALANQUIN

As the Camellia-style rehabilitation model started to gain validation, I decided to start another similar experiment with a furniture franchise. For if we succeeded in pulling half a million children from the Indian slums, that would still leave millions behind. Palanquin, our furniture brand, became this second major rehabilitation project.

This time, since the products under development were not perishable, we no longer needed the centers to be in close proximity to major, highly populated cities. As a result, we were able to even further optimize on real estate costs. Where for Camellia we paid on average Rs. 1.5 lakhs (~$3,000) for an acre, the land for Palanquin cost only Rs. 0.5 lakhs (~$1,000).

It would seem a chore to find sections of land broad enough to hold our dormitories and schoolhouses, as well as this time both workshops and land to grow bamboo at a large scale, but India remained land rich. Many farmers who owned plots of agricultural land had not been able to grow enough, nor monetize adequately their holdings. And after years of toil, they were willing to sell at the attractive prices we offered.

Financing also became easier as we had established strong inroads with Asian Development Bank and IFC, as well as our numerous microfinance bank relationships. And so we built, one by one, Palanquin centers to which the kids came, wide-eyed first, then gradually settling into a rhythm of meticulous work, weaving the seats of cane armchairs, looking up at times to smile at a watching instructor.

The difference we did face, and it was a major one, was in the development and workflow of a furniture brand. Following my instinct about design, we engaged Japanese designers to work with us twice a year on a core set of designs, delivered as 3-D files. They were elegant designs with poetic curvatures, moving fluidly with the lightness of bamboo, the inherent presence of teak. From these specifications we built sofa sets, coffee tables, beds, dining tables and chairs, armchairs, stools, lamps, desks, chests, showcases, and almirahs. In 2009, over sawdust and the rich smell of cut wood, I saw the first prototype of a coffee table in the Akalpoush workshop. It had invoked Isamu Noguchi's 1944 design of a free-form plate glass top with a self-stabilizing base made of two interlocking pieces of wood. The excitement in the kids' eyes, their obvious thrill at giving form to what they saw on the computer screen, assured me we were on the right path.

The positioning for the brand was *affordable elegance*. Design within reach, so to speak. I had observed Target's successful introduction of design-based differentiation into the mass retail category in the US, and with Palanquin that was what I intended to achieve. But instead of catering to the US middle class, we would serve the quickly expanding Indian middle class. Our prices, therefore, were deliberately pegged at attainable levels. Not only could high-flying software executives afford them, but call center managers could, professors could, and even Thakur chefs were taking home our wares.

In terms of distribution, we decided to build the first eight Palanquin stores ourselves before franchising the retail concept. This way, for each region, we had a model store up and running, which the franchisees were able to then replicate in design and user experience. Here too, located in many of the Green Village apartment complexes and shopping malls, accessing a ready clientele, we went with a minimalist Japanese design – an open, softly lit floor plan with islands of concepts framed in paper screens.

By 2012, we had 80 stores. Each sold on average 10,000 units of furniture to some 2,500 families, generating $500,000 in annual revenue. Combined, our 2012 revenue totaled $40 million. A good start, but by 2015 we had grown to 650 stores. Walking by windows on summer evenings, one would see living room after living room embellished with Palanquin pieces. We had become a near monopoly in our segment of affordable designer furniture. Revenues touched $300 million.

Our kids, meanwhile, were not only getting savvy in building beautiful, high-quality furniture, they were starting to play with CAD software, learning to design their own products. Think3, an Italian CAD vendor I had worked with as a consultant back in 2002, donated software for each of our centers. Soon, the labs developed waiting lines of kids who had stopped going out and goofing around to start competing among themselves, designing.

What we couldn't have expected came in 2016. In our center at Shantiniketan, a truly talented resident designer, Chameli Rai, emerged with the design of a dining set accentuating the natural grain and texture of wood. There was an understated and unexpected confidence in her concept that made me frown. We invited her to design a new line, but it was the market that made her a star.

By 2018, we no longer needed to outsource Japanese designers. Indigenous designers sprouted up at several centers, especially Champaner and Shantiniketan. Soon we had more market-worthy designs than we knew what to do with. But even among them, there were those that separated themselves. Folding screens with painted murals became a form of contemporary art that we popularized.

In 2019, *BusinessWeek* honored Chameli Rai's armchair with a Product Design of the Year award. Its effortless honoring of wood drove the market with a sex appeal the Apple iPod once had. Almost immediately we found ourselves unable to keep them in stock – so quickly were they going out in delivery trucks or in the backs of customers' cars, for home.

Today in 2020, with revenue touching a billion dollars, with 2,000 stores spanning 300 cities, towns, and townships, and Palanquin furniture gracing almost every Indian living room, we have built from wood and cane, and sweat and pride, one of the leading furniture manufacturers in the world. Some 500,000 workers would have to be gathered to show the full breadth of our achievements. No picture could capture all of them, or the reversal of their lives and the skills they've built themselves on. All of them gathered as one, and one of them, Chameli Rai, standing as the culmination of all. Her story, which travels from lip to lip through the Indian slums, is one of raw talent and defiant originality. She is no lucky "slumdog millionaire." For if luck had anything to do with her story, it was only in her parents' decision to enroll her in the Palanquin experiment.

DEEPTI

Having honed our methodology with the 12 to 18 age group, moving them out of city slums, providing them education and viable professional skills, I started to expand on the idea. For with the success we were witnessing among the 12 to 18 year olds, it was impossible to watch the rest of their families continue to struggle amidst the slum squalor. I wondered if we could go further, moving entire families. Deepti was the first project to test this direction.

As we expanded the scope of our market research, we heard again and again, "We would love to move out of the city, but we have nowhere to go." For most, the city, no matter its brutal pace, its pollution, and violence, held better opportunities than the village. One particular 36-year-old mother of three who had moved to Kolkata from a rural town added immense color to our research. She worked as a maid servicing five different households. "You work all day long in the field, but can't even afford two meals," she said. "Here, my income is good. Although, where we live is terrible. I miss our village home." In the city, her husband worked as a rickshaw puller, earning 200 rupees, or $4 a day. Enough to feed the family's five mouths, but nothing more.

I chose candles for the Deepti project because they're easy to make, non-perishable, and boasted an enormous global market of $15 billion in 2008. I estimated this to grow to almost $80 billion by 2020. And with innovative designs, we could produce something unique and differentiated, experimenting with exotic forms and shapes, as well as fragrance.

To start this project, we first had to create a place for the slum dwellers to go. Leaving the city behind, we looked at land adjacent to land we'd already acquired for Camellia and Palanquin. Here we acquired large chunks of land – ten acres apiece – and in these untouched fields, we broke ground on low-cost housing for about 5,000–6,000 people per. These Deepti centers overlooked fields of irises owned by Camellia and sprawled near the workshops of Palanquin. When the Vidyangan school hours ended, the children spread out in the fields and hurried into their respective shops, making candles and armchairs and futures.

In the beginning, we used the same model as Camellia: inner-city sales reps empowered with Deepti franchises selling door-to-door, offering strings of dark indigo non-drip candles to the upwardly mobile. These reps told the story of their craftsmen and their valiant effort toward a better future. Customers stood in doorways listening. Their children popped their heads out occasionally, fingering the candles where they hung. With a large portion of the Indian middle class's household incomes now between $30,000 and $60,000 a year, and the cost of living still relatively low, the affluent could spare $25 a year to support the candle-makers.

And they did. Gradually, candles began illuminating affluent dinner parties and events. Whole tables of biryani and parathas jittered in the wavering light. They also lit altars, a place where only flowers and oil lamps – *pradeeps* – had had a place before.

We started selling candles to hotels and spas, including Amrapali, Renaissance, and Darjeeling. These corporate deals ensured us important working capital as we juggled the various challenges of a rather complex enterprise relocating families, building communities, and rebuilding livelihoods.

By the end of 2011, we had 60 centers – each franchised by a regional entrepreneur – in which 80,000 people found an opportunity to restart their lives. This time, as they returned to village life, there was a livelihood awaiting them. We produced 12 million candles that year, and most importantly, we did so while preserving perfection in every contour. Our 2011 revenue was modest at $6 million.

In 2012, with a reasonable operation in place, we started exporting to reach a broader market with bigger margins. While in Palanquin, exports would have been cumbersome due to the more complex packaging and shipping requirements, candles were relatively simple to work with. In light of this, we created an e-commerce business to cater to North America and Europe, where we could undercut prices by a third. Beyond our price differentiation, our story which we told on our Web site – that Deepti was offering thousands of slum dwellers a better opportunity – generated tremendous consumer interest from the West.

Our international footing soon took hold. By 2015, we had 1.3 million online customers and $200 million in export revenue. The domestic business, meanwhile, had grown to $100 million. The following year, we began marketing to restaurants, hotels, and spas – to those with bulk needs – in Europe and North America. In fact, the hotels, restaurants, and spas further spread the Deepti brand deep into their customer base. And soon, with households following the commercial trend, business grew rapidly – our revenue scaled to $300 million in export, while domestic followed suit to the tune of $150 million.

Amazingly, we had taken a commodity product and turned it into a status symbol both by giving it aesthetic appeal, and by making affluent people all over the world feel responsible for our anti-slum movement. We were, lit by our candles, enjoying what economists call the "warm glow effect" – that many products are bought because they make people feel good about themselves.

The global media gave us a huge hand in spreading the movement. Photojournalists captured disturbing images of maimed slum children in Kolkata, Mumbai, Delhi, and Lucknow, and as they wrote about them, they also wrote extensively about the alternatives that projects such as Deepti, Camellia, and Palanquin were creating. Contrasting images of shanties against idyllic candle-making communities in rural India captured the imagination of the world.

But unlike many such endeavors, we were not a nonprofit. We were a thriving, triple bottom-line enterprise serving our shareholders, alongside our local communities and the greater environment. Our reward: In 2020, our projected revenue is close to a billion dollars; our 1,500 Deepti centers are home to some two million former slum dwellers; and our four million online customers spread across North America and Europe, from Santa Barbara to Calgary, Cardiff to Cannes, Rome to Munich, lighting the globe from one window to the next.

GAGORI

Even during the early success of Deepti, I could see that the project would not scale to move more than a couple million people out of the cities. I needed more projects like it, and I came up with Gagori as a second, focusing on relocation of entire families from city to village.

Depressing statistics were coming in from the slums at a fantastic pace. Even a relatively smaller city like Lucknow – let alone Mumbai, Kolkata, or Delhi – had 750 slums in 2009. The scale of the problem was absolutely staggering, as were the results – crime, alcoholism, drugs, skyrocketing rates of mental illness, even suicide. And with such unbridled urban expansion, it was easy to project a pressure-cooker future for India's already horrendously congested infrastructure.

In 2009, a *Wall Street Journal* article forecasted Mumbai's population to cross 20 million in 2010, and 26 million in 2025. Delhi would cross 20 million in 2020, and Kolkata in 2025. Bangalore, Hyderabad, Chennai, Pune, Ludhiana, Patna, and another ten mega-cities were each bursting at their seams with overflowing traffic, substandard sewage infrastructure, and a thick cloud of doomsday-esque carbon dioxide.

In *Humanity's Environmental Future: Making Sense in a Troubled World*, author William Ross McCluney posed the question: How many people can the earth really support? McCluney's answer: between 500 million and one billion, at a reasonable standard of living. Ecologist and agronomist David Pimentel of Cornell University found similar numbers. By hypothetically extending the 2008 average standard of living of US citizens to all people in the world, his research showed that the earth's carrying capacity is inadequate to support a world population of over one to two billion people.

So there I was, sitting with a computer, a spreadsheet, some market research, and an anxious intellect. The problem we faced: we needed to move at least four billion people to another planet. Or, without such a second planetary option, we needed to redistribute the population over the land we had, and in so much reimagine the possibilities of now underutilized ground.

Gagori followed much of the same principles of Deepti. We acquired large tracts of land – tens of acres – and built 1,500-person communities, and by 2020, we had 1,500 of them laboring away far, far from the cities. In picturesque settings, our former slum-dwelling inhabitants spent their days working on pottery wheels, solar-powered kilns, and such, building beautiful platters, bowls, tea sets, and vases.

Gagori, of course, had a significant design element to it, for which I wrestled briefly with Indian designers, but I was unable to get the level of simplicity I sought. Consequently, I resigned to using Japanese and Italian designers alongside Indian ones, slowly shaping their tastes and instincts. This was a very important decision since a substantial export business was crucial to making the Gagori numbers interesting. We had to cater to Western taste, and that palette would not accept designs as complex as what the Indian designers kept bringing to the table.

For the domestic market, we accessed another important lever: Palanquin stores were perfect outlets for Gagori products. The two brands complemented each other, deftly balancing Gagori platters on Palanquin dining tables, catering to the same core audience. We were able to sell $200 million worth of Gagori merchandise through the Palanquin stores in 2015.

The export business, as I envisioned, was twice that size, although our projections show a 50:50 pairing by 2025.

Gagori, as a brand, has developed tremendous international appeal. In this case, we have not only been able to differentiate with pricing, delivering the absolute highest quality pottery at 25% of the price of Western comparables, but we've also set ourselves apart at a purely product level. In fact, we did not tell the slum rehabilitation story at all in building this brand. Since Gagori's products had much higher differentiation potential based on design and pricing, we felt no need to play the additional card of the rehabilitation story, which commodity products like candles needed more acutely.

An early deal with Design Within Reach gave us huge leverage on this front. DWR carries for the most part, Scandinavian, Japanese, and Italian designers. Our late-blooming Indian designers found their vases among the legends – the Eameses, the Mendinis, the Castiglionis, and the Wegners, which then led us to other major retail partnerships with Williams-Sonoma and eventually Target, each of which became huge channels. Of course, for Target, we developed a separate line under a new brand, Gargi, without diluting the brand equity in the high-end line.

In fact, we returned the early favor to Palanquin by introducing them to all three retailers, and they too were able to leverage the relationships and access substantial additional revenues. Deepti, as well, found prime additional channels for its candles.

As I look back on Gagori's last decade, two things make me very proud. One, predictably, is the fact that we have moved another two million slum dwellers out of the Indian cities such that they live today in clean, decent housing, their children watching as their hands maneuver lumps of moist clay on pottery wheels. The second, I must admit, is my sheer delight at the quality of design and finish we have achieved in the Gagori products. The India Inc. brand, once characterized by cheap, low-quality, poorly-designed products, now, once and for all, has shed that humiliating stigma.

PATAMI

As I looked deeper into India's natural strengths, jute emerged as a mainstay. This easy-to-grow, rain-fed crop with little need for fertilizer or pesticides had been used for everything from sacks to ropes since the British set up the first jute mill in Rishra in 1855.

India dominated world production, holding 66% market share. Bangladesh came next with 25%. Quite a strong foothold – and quite a promising one. Jute is second only to cotton as the world's most important vegetable fiber. So, in 2009, we established Patami, a brand of home furnishing products with jute at the center, spinning yarns of carpets, curtains, and upholstery.

We opened the project with multiple components: First, we established supplier relationships with various jute mills throughout the Gangetic plains, which spanned West Bengal and Bangladesh, the breadbasket if you will of jute production. Second, we established relationships with two key microfinance institutions, Bandhan in India, and Grameen Bank in Bangladesh, to offer enterprise loans to Patami franchisees who had already gone through one or two loan cycles with the MFI. Next, we needed to address the design, merchandising, and marketing issues.

While traveling in Santa Fe, New Mexico, I'd seen Navajo rugs and blankets commanding prices in the range of $1,200 to $1,500. At Chimayo, a Navajo artisan was selling his rugs for $2,300 to $2,500. But I did not want Patami furnishings to be priced above $50. Instead, we created a line of affordable jute furnishings that the affluent, yet price-conscious, Indian consumers would happily add to their homes.

But what of design? After all, how could a woman who had never ventured outside her small village of Kamalakantapur even begin to imagine what an upper-class career woman living in a Bangalore high-rise might look for, let alone a housewife in Manhattan? When they tried, the results were often overworked, cluttering their designs, cramming in more where less would have sufficed.

All this I knew firsthand, having traveled throughout rural India, having spoken with villagers about design, manufacturing, and marketing their merchandise, and having interacted with numerous well-meaning NGO workers trying to bridge the gap. The problem was that even the social workers did not have the design, merchandising, or marketing savvy. Specialized expertise was called for, and on my trip to Cambodia in 2008, I found the answer. Artisans d'Ankor, a joint venture between the French and Cambodian governments, had achieved what numerous design/marketing-oriented efforts in India needed to replicate. And they did so by employing French designers to work with the local artisans, preserving their craft while offering the necessary refinement.

And so I returned to my tried-and-true formula of working with European and Japanese designers. In fact, in 2009, France was facing an unemployment rate of 9.8%. Dominique and I had spent a week in Paris in July that year. It was heartbreaking to see the normally bustling cafés and restaurants unthinkably empty. As we enjoyed a splendid lunch of escargots de Bourgogne and moules mariniére at the Auberge de la Reine Blanche in Ile de Saint-Louis, only two of the 12 tables were occupied. A small Basque perfumerie in Place de Vosges looked precariously desolate. A florist in the Marais sat waiting.

The French, I knew, loved to travel, and they especially loved Asia due to their imperialistic history in Indochina. With this in mind, we recruited designers from France to come work in India and Bangladesh, side by side with the artisans. Young, talented designers in search of life experience applied in the thousands to our online job listings. In total, we reviewed 10,000 portfolios, of which we interviewed 1,000 in Paris. We eventually hired 100 French designers to work with 1,000 Patami franchisees, producing simple, sophisticated, high-quality jute carpets, curtains, cushions, wall hangings, bedspreads, and blankets. They had varied backgrounds. Some were trained at Pont-Aven in Brittany, some at Marangoni in Paris, and still others at La Cambre in Brussels.

To launch, we looked first to Palanquin furniture stores. Within two years, we were in 40 branches across India – cane armchairs reclined on dark red jute carpets with black weavings, at the feet of a perfectly segmented customer base of upwardly mobile Indians. In fact, in 10 years, our Palanquin channel alone grew to almost $100 million. But we did not settle there. We also sold through Fab India, another major distribution channel that brought us excellent coverage through their less spacious but extremely popular stores. And in 2012, we also negotiated a very large distribution deal with Scandinavian home décor magnate IKEA. By the time our deal kicked into gear, they had 400 stores crossing Europe, America, and Asia.

No longer was our challenge about getting to market; we faced a different challenge. We had to scale our production side exponentially from 1,000 franchisees to 10,000 by 2013. Both Bandhan and Grameen were delighted to help us face the problem on the financing side, and our access to European designers sustained nicely. As a result, we continued to scale the model, and by 2015, we had 100,000 Patami franchisees weaving for us throughout West Bengal and Bangladesh.

It was an interesting experiment, employing Europeans in rural South Asia. The living arrangements were quite basic, and they certainly weren't offered fois gras for dinner. Food, in fact, was simple, rural Bengali cuisine, and yet, the designers salivated over the dal and basmati rice, boiled spinach sprinkled with mustard oil, and fried hilsa. On average, they would spend three to five years with the company, taking the time to learn the culture, soak up the beauty of the countryside, and seek within for answers to their existential questions!

An existential question that the West was facing at large was, "How much do you need to be happy?" Well, living side by side with the Patami franchisees exposed them to a way of life that was at once joyful and minimalist, fulfilling and provincial. A cow tethered to the pole of one's courtyard furnished the morning glass of milk. Eggs came fresh from the chicken in the yard. Some vegetables came from the patch along the side of the house. What would seem like not much turned out to be more than enough.

The reputation of the program spread to the American design schools, and soon students from RISD, CCA, Parsons, and others joined our French Patami team in droves. Middle-American tastes started infiltrating the product lines, granting us followings in Texas and Arizona. Less Asian, more Navajo.

Meanwhile, the Patami franchisees experienced a remarkable increase in their household income. Groups of women who had risen from dire poverty came together in village after village to weave and embroider. SELCO, a solar energy company run by my friend Harish Hande, installed solar lights for them to work by at night. And work they did, without worry of either design or marketing – each substantial bottlenecks in their limited, provincial existence.

And jute, once Bengal's pride and Bangladesh's joy, reinstated itself in the hearts of the riverine people along the Ganges-Brahmaputra Delta.

VIDYANGAN

Every year, in the fall, the MIT Club of Northern California holds its flagship event in the Bay Area. In 2008, the guest of honor was Nicholas Negroponte, formerly director of the MIT Media Lab, and most famously, creator of the One Laptop Per Child (OLPC) endeavor.

I spoke with Negroponte about the goals of his project, chronicling the OLPC story for *Forbes*. OLPC, which Negroponte founded in 2005, had sent 5,000 laptops to Ethiopia, 10,000 to Rwanda, 8,000 to Haiti, and 10,000 to Mongolia – to name just a few countries, and only the first three years of work. By the end of 2008, the organization was expecting to put nearly one million laptops in the hands of needy children all over the world. "Our focus is not the next billion, but the *last* billion," Negroponte said, referring to the world's poorest people.

As I listened to him, ideas began to float into my head about how to roll out a scalable education system in the heartland of India, down to the poorest of the poor. Maybe not the last billion, but certainly the next billion.

OLPC had five core tenets: (a) private ownership, instead of school ownership; (b) low ages, with both hardware and software designed for elementary school children, aged 6–12; (c) saturation, instead of random sprinkling in disjointed geographies; (d) connection; and (e) free and open source. The OLPC laptops were to be sold to governments and then distributed to children by education ministries.

While I took much from OLPC in terms of ideas and architectural underpinnings, the Vidyangan school project was not based on the same principles as OLPC. For example, our laptops were owned by the schools, and our initial target was middle school and high school students, whom our slum rehabilitation partners Camellia, Gagori, Deepti, and others were quickly moving to rural India. While these companies provided the school buildings, all schools on their premises throughout India were to be run by Vidyangan. Our goal: use low-cost connected laptops to teach middle school and high school curriculum, from literacy and languages, to math and sciences, as well as history and geography. Thus, a large part of our emphasis was on creating the right immersive software and digital content.

In a 10-year window, Vidyangan was designed to educate three million kids in the 12–18 age group.

There was a slight hitch, though. The families of these students could not afford to pay tuition, which meant we needed to come up with a creative solution to support these schools from a revenue point of view. Here we looked to the Vidyangan laptops themselves. While on school premises, the laptops were fully networked, connected to the Internet, the world at a touch of a button. But beyond our schoolhouses, Internet access, and through it world access, was an elusive creature. With this in mind, we created a program for India's top brands like Nirma, Liril, and LifeBuoy to advertize through the laptops, reaching previously untouched consumers in rural India. Yes, our ad-supported Vidyangan school system required that for up to five hours per week, the students would go out to their surrounding rural territory, with their laptops, and show the villagers video clips, acting as brand ambassadors.

In this way, each Vidyangan school supported almost 300,000 brand conversation slots a year. In ten years, the Vidyangan school system had created over three billion brand conversation slots, with over 500 million of those slots supported by our partners, Camellia, Gagori, and Deepti. With each slot priced at Rs. 25 (50 cents), we had $1.6 billion in ad inventory by 2020. And with a 70% sell-through rate, we achieved a billion dollars in annual revenue.

Armed with this unique business model, the job of educating three million underprivileged kids moved from the unthinkable to the undeniable. We tackled a great deal of the teaching with standardized software and content provided by the school system. In the heartland of India, finding great teachers was not easy, so we tackled a good 90% of the content knowledge in software, and we used the "teachers" to manage and orchestrate the classrooms, focusing on supported self-learning.

While all our kids learned the exact same material, their minds were also opened expansively to Internet research and self-guided exploration, so that each child also developed his or her own unique point of view. This resulted in some interesting dynamics. In a school in Sikkim, the kids were studying the Himalayas in geography class. In particular, they were learning about Tibet. As they started digging around on the Internet, some discovered articles on China's human rights violations. Others discovered an article on my Web site about Tibet being the source of several of the greatest water sources in Asia, and that China wanted to control Tibet for that reason. The discussions and debates that ensued were animated and not in the least bit off topic. Our curriculum was designed to allow for such independent exploration assignments through which not only did the students learn, but so did their teachers, for such abundant Internet access was also new to them.

Vidyangan's success in gaining widespread adoption of networked laptops attracted a large number of educational software companies to get into the market. We partnered with many of them, affording them the three million sets of eyes and ears we were educating. Very soon, in fact, our software- and content-related R&D dropped to zero as the ecosystem of companies around us began delivering the pieces we needed, filling the gaps as we identified them.

We also encouraged developing an engaged political consciousness in our students. Unlike most schools in India, Vidyangan students were encouraged to participate in political activism, striving for an educated, aware nation. As the BJP tried to spread a message of Hindu nationalism, our students read about Akbar's Dīn-i Ilāhī and debated the dangers of Islamic fundamentalism. Their teachers encouraged discussions about the philosophical underpinnings of a variety of religions. And the secular philosophy upon which the constitution of independent India was based received thorough back and forth, as did Mahatma Gandhi's role in the India-Pakistan mess. No stone went unturned – in fact, altogether new stones were discovered and rolled about by student and teacher alike.

Over time, Vidyangan became the single largest school in the world, with over 10,000 networked campuses. We could not only make or break brands through our reach of over 30 million consumers, we also held the power to spread ideas, develop movements, and build leaders. In fact, one of the early team members of Vidyangan, who started off as a high school teacher in a small village in Uttaranchal – an idealistic, inspiring 30-year-old in 2010 – went on to become the education minister of India in 2019. And as he developed political capital, we helped him spread the message of an educated India, a productive India, an enlightened India – far and wide.

AMRAKUNJA

As we continued our slum rehabilitation projects, moving people out into rural India, we also started working on turning hectares of slums into mango groves. Square in the middle of rising cities.

In doing so, we linked up with the European Commission for a carbon-trading project. The United Nations' afforestation efforts are managed by its Clean Development Mechanism (CDM). The CDM governing committee first decides if a project qualifies for carbon credits, then the number of credits to be allocated. Officially known as Certified Emission Reduction (CER) credits, each is equivalent to one ton of carbon dioxide, and they are bought and sold in specialized international exchanges. Developed countries use them towards meeting their mandatory greenhouse gas reduction targets under the Kyoto Protocol.

We took a worldview in raising funds for the project. Our ambition: convert slum lands in Kolkata, Mumbai, Delhi, Bangalore, Hyderabad, Chennai, and Ahmedabad into green landscapes full of mango trees. The Carbon Finance arm of the World Bank helped us pull together €230 million ($300 million) towards this ambition from several carbon funds in Italy, Spain, Netherlands, Denmark, Norway, France, and Belgium. This was further enhanced with contributions by seven state governments (Maharashtra, West Bengal, Tamil Nadu, Haryana, Andhra Pradesh, Karnataka, and Gujarat) totaling another €70 million. So our project, to be carried out in 7,000 slums in seven cities over a five-year period, was off and running.

There was already a concerted effort towards moving children and families out of the slums in several cities through projects like Camellia, Deepti, Palanquin, and Gagori – so location was never an issue. As slums emptied into the heartland of India, into cleaner, healthier settings, amidst fields of irises and carnations, they left behind what we began to refer to as our own urban fields.

With entire slums of people relocated, the landlords could sell their lands to us. In fact, many of them had wanted to sell for years, but due to India's convoluted legal system, they had been unable to evict their tenants. Now they could, and without the kind of anarchy that had often been the byproduct of major land acquisition efforts in the past. One of the worst of these had been the Singur project in which the Tatas had wanted to set up a Nano factory. Nearly 1,000 acres of land was needed, but the relocation of the people had not been adequately prepared. This gave Trinamul Congress leader Mamata Banerjee a perfect opportunity to create precisely the kind of anarchy she excelled in. Banerjee proclaimed that she would not budge from her stand of demanding the 400 acres of land taken for the Tata Nano project in Singur. Events went out of control. A young girl was burnt alive. Banerjee herself went on a hunger strike. Finally, the Tatas pulled out and abandoned their plans to set up a factory in West Bengal.

Amrakunja did not make any such blunder. Our collaboration was tightly woven with the other projects moving slum dwellers towards better futures. In our media relations too, we clearly articulated that we were not forcibly acquiring land, rather, that our project was a piece of the overall slum rehabilitation puzzle that was gaining excellent goodwill through the efforts of Camellia, Gagori, and others.

Slum by slum, block by block, the Amrakunja team went about acquiring parcels of land and demolishing shabby, poorly constructed buildings. In some cases, the last remaining inhabitants were offered alternative accommodation that was of substantially higher quality. Once the leveling of makeshift houses was completed, the ground had to be cleaned and then opened deep to make room for rich soil. It was this rich soil that our midsized mango trees found waiting in the city's shade.

By 2015, each of the seven cities had turned substantially greener, and in the summer, the aroma of luscious mangoes won out over the stench from the drains. We had, of course, seen this coming, and prepared for it. Amrakunja-branded mangoes – Himsagar, Alfonso, Lyangra, and numerous other juicy and fragrant varietals – filled the markets, generating an additional revenue stream besides the carbon trading grants. Meanwhile, people came to walk among the tress, sit on benches in their shade, and rejuvenate their spirits.

By 2018, the number of slums we had transitioned into mango groves touched 20,000, and by 2020, 35,000. We had $1.5 billion in carbon trading dollars under management, and we were also producing a very significant amount of high-quality mangoes, some of which were used domestically or exported in pickles, chutneys, jams, juices, and other preserves.

I never thought mangoes would once again become such an important part of my life. But here they were woven into the cities, just as they were into my childhood memories. Having grown up in Kolkata, I cannot recall summer without mangoes. My grandfather owned mango orchards in Rajarhat, where he experimented for years cross-pollinating different varietals. Consequently, all summer, mangoes arrived at our Elgin Road house – first on bullock carts, and later, by bus – from the orchards. We feasted five times a day. From mango ice cream to mango pickle, our palettes and senses, from May through July, overflowed with mangoes.

That all ended in 1989, when I left for college in the United States. Gradually, as I stopped coming to India during the summer, choosing instead the more pleasant winter months for my visits, mangoes all but departed my life. When I saw the afforestation opportunity, I couldn't help but build the project around these lost mangoes.

Ten years into the project, a bird's-eye view of an Indian metro looks vastly different from what it did in 2010. The percentage of lush green treetops among the roofs has taken a striking leap forward. Today, when my plane lands, I look out upon a true urban jungle, except this one is no longer solely of concrete. This one's air breathes cleaner; this one's sky burns brighter.

HIM-ICON

Springboarding off our Amrakunja successes, I began to look further into the state of Indian agriculture. In 2003, the Indian agriculture sector accounted for 26% of the country's GDP, producing 64% of the nation's employment. Globally, India stood as the second largest producer of fruits and vegetables in the world, and the second-largest vegetable exporter. A 2003 report suggested that out of 370 million tons of fruit produced in the world, India accounted for 30 million tons, and of the 456 million tons of vegetable, India's share was 59 million tons, or 17%. Yet, India's share was only 1% of the world's trade in fruits and vegetables. How was this possible? A tremendous volume of post-harvest wastage was diminishing the country's productivity.

Much of this loss was caused by the lack of well-thought-through refrigerated storage. Another hindrance lay in India's poor transportation infrastructure. Whatever the cause, India's perishable products were perishing in too great a number.

The wastage was estimated at 25% of total produce, or approximately Rs. 50,000 crores ($10 billion). In other words, without any investment into production volume, addressing these rudimentary logistical issues could result in monetization worth an additional $10 billion.

Sounds simple enough: refrigerators, trucks, and improved management. However, agriculture in India remained extremely decentralized with over 75% small-scale, cottage industry–style fruit and vegetable processing units. Local cold storages had limited capacity, so farmers often found themselves with fields of almost ripe tomatoes but no room in the cold storage. This meant, in another week, the entire field would rot. Few farmers had the financial staying power to withstand such devastation. Yet, few cold storage owners had the business savvy to gauge the region's full production capacity and do sophisticated yield management, constructing new facilities to support the region in its entirety.

Our Him-Icon venture set out to link up thousands of small and large producers to international retailers and other wholesale buyers through a network of cold-storage facilities, refrigerated containers, and terminals that enabled perishable produce to be stored and transported by road, rail, river, and sea. Him-Icon, in a nutshell, became the largest fruits and vegetable exporter and distributor in India.

We established trusted partnerships with 2,500-plus producers across 10 states – Maharashtra, Gujarat, Karnataka, Andhra Pradesh, Tamil Nadu, Orissa, Madhya Pradesh, Uttar Pradesh, Bihar, and West Bengal – by helping them access loans from microfinance banks. In the past, these farmers had often defaulted on their loan payments when they were unable to sell perishable produce on time. However, by identifying themselves as partners of Him-Icon, they were able to address the monetization concerns of their financiers. These farmers, by working with us, began expanding their businesses by 50% every year, which the banks were more than happy to finance.

In terms of production, we focused on three broad categories: mangoes, onions, and grapes.

The major mango-growing states in India were Andhra Pradesh, Uttar Pradesh, West Bengal, Maharashtra, Gujarat, and Karnataka. The total mango export from India in 2008 was 54,350 metric tons, a value of Rs. 127.42 crores ($25 million). For years, the major export destinations were the Emirates, UK, Bangladesh, Nepal, and Saudi Arabia, but we saw no reason not to expand into European and American markets, while also growing our presence in the Middle East. So, by 2010, we developed a mango export business worth $25 million. By 2015, the business grew to $50 million, and in 2020 we will export $124 million worth of mangoes – primarily to the Middle East, Western Europe, and North America.

The second in our three-pronged Him-Icon business was onions. In 2008, the major onion-producing states – Maharashtra, Gujarat, Uttar Pradesh, Orissa, Karnataka, Tamil Nadu, Madhya Pradesh, Andhra Pradesh, and Bihar – exported a total of Rs. 1035 crores ($217 million). By 2010, we managed to develop a $35 million onion business, primarily by growing our Middle Eastern and Malaysian markets, which were already strong importers of Indian onions. The major onion export destinations were Bangladesh, Malaysia, UAE, Sri Lanka, and Nepal, of which, the Middle East had the best margins. The onion business grew rapidly to $130 million by 2015, and it is forecasted to hit $500 million in 2020.

Finally, for our grape business we chose a specialty market: wine. In 2008, and for years before, India's grape exports had stagnated around the Netherlands, UK, Bangladesh, UAE, and Germany. We wanted to reinvent this. So, instead of exporting our grapes, we developed a partnership with Constellation Wines, one of the largest wine companies in the world, who were eager to enter the Indian market. And enter it they did. Constellation brought winemakers from its top global brands. Brands like Franciscan, Robert Mondavi, Mount Veeder, Simi, and Estancia of California; Columbia Winery of Washington State; Ruffino of Tuscany; Kim Crawford and Drylands of Marlborough, New Zealand; and Tintara of McLaren Vale, Australia. They came with their own experts, setting up wineries with their carefully guarded manufacturing processes among the vineyards of Maharashtra and Karnataka. They built cellars, set up fermentation equipment, and soon, new labels produced with Indian grapes based on manufacturing processes of these masters started showing up at restaurants and newly popular wine bars.

Grapes from Maharashtra, Karnataka, Andhra Pradesh, and Tamil Nadu boomed to a $112 million business for us by 2015, and $280 million in 2020, as we became the primary supplier for Constellation and others including the Wine Group, Bronco, and Foster's.

Our hub-and-spoke model, with 25 refrigerated terminals strategically located in the 10 states where we did business, was an undeniable success. Our fleet of air-conditioned trucks picked up merchandise from regional producers and delivered it to the closest of the container terminals on a daily basis. The mango and onion containers moved by rail to the nearest port, while the grape containers were transported directly to local wineries. In addition, we developed a cold storage chain, supplying regional storage to fulfill longer storage requirements.

Today, a computer simulation of our network shows how the trucks, trains, and ships spread across India, reaping the full rewards these markets once failed to achieve.

COWHERD CREAMERY

As I began thinking about projects for rural India that fit the micro-franchise business model, one idea really captured my imagination. Over my decades in the United States, and through a rather intimate exposure to European cultures, I had become quite accustomed to good cheese – something sorely missing in India.

In fact, the middle-class Indian consumer had, in most cases, never even been introduced to the taste of good cheese. They used to think Amul was the epitome of great cheese. Amul, in 2008, was jointly owned by some five million milk producers in Gujarat. It had been a wildly successful dairy brand, but the cooperative most certainly had no idea what gourmet cheese was. La Tur, for example, one of my all-time favorites, is a blend of cow, sheep, and goat milk. Pasteurized at the lowest temperature allowed by law, it retains much of the flavors of unpasteurized cheeses. Kirk Samuels explained La Tur in *365 Cheeses*: "The best way to describe it is like butter with an attitude. At the proper temperature and ripeness it is soft, smooth, and spreadable but still dense with pungent, ripe flavor. It is sold in small, four-inch disks about one inch deep placed in pleated paper like a cupcake." Indeed, it is its own sort of cupcake, for adults.

What if we created a cheese franchise that villagers all over India could participate in? What if we trained thousands of artisan cheesemakers to rival the quality of La Tur, Humboldt Fog, Explorateur, Parmigiano Reggiano, and Saint Agur?

As I researched this idea, I was surprised to learn that cheese, in fact, was invented in Asia. It was discovered accidentally by an Arab merchant who put his reserve of milk into a sheepskin pouch as he journeyed across the desert. The rennet in the lining of the pouch, combined with the heat of the desert sun, caused the milk to separate into curd and whey. This curd came to be known as cheese. And this cheese arrived in Europe by way of Asian travelers, most likely on horseback.

Now in India, cow, goat, buffalo, and sheep were abundantly available, some even meandering through the congested traffic of Mumbai and Kolkata – their milk awaiting the magic touch of experienced cheesemakers. And as the milk awaited cheesemakers, so too did the Asian continent as a whole.

We also realized that since high-end cheese was not a product that Indian consumers knew a whole lot about, they needed education, which meant we had to market the brand as a hip phenomenon, elevating it above simple food product to an essential lifestyle product. Luckily, wine was becoming more popular, and of course wine and cheese were, once brought together, inseparable.

Another important piece once missing from the Indian market was an efficient refrigerated transportation network to ensure that cheese produced in the heartland of India would make it to retail stores in the cities without spoiling. Of course, this was being addressed by Him-Icon, as well as Magic Carpet Roads and Lightning Rails.

To begin our venture we looked to Dominique's childhood friend, Philippe Demortier, a longtime player in the Belgian gourmet food and wine business. Philippe knew cheesemakers in France, Holland, and Switzerland, and he took us to meet several of Europe's most revered. As I ate at their tables and drank their fine wines, I began to inquire about the process of cheese making. What was so special about aging cheeses? Finally, I explained what I had in mind – at first tentatively, then once they'd opened their dairies, their milking barns, and their curdling and aging areas to me, we talked through the night.

At the end of the trip, we sent a team of 20 aspiring Indian cheesemakers to study with masters in France, Italy, Switzerland, and Holland. In parallel, we invited a small group of five masters to come to India and create their own lines of cheeses under the Cowherd Creamery brand. They created a fine range of cheeses reminiscent of a Tuscan Mozzarella di Bufala, a Dutch Parrano, and a French St. Marcellin. Meanwhile, the 20 Indians learned firsthand the details and subtleties of cheese making in Europe.

By 2010, we had the process and recipe for 40 new artisan cheeses, some created by the European masters, and some by our team of Indian cheesemakers. So with the recipes in hand, we built our first 10 rural cheese factories.

For customers, instead of going immediately to retail, we lined up 1,000 high-end hotels all across India as our primary market. We knew it would take time to educate the consumers, making a retail channel viable. But hotels with ready high-end clientele were already seeing a strong adoption of wine, and they could easily introduce an elegant cheese platter with 6–10 different Cowherd Creamery cheeses. Besides, they had the staff to educate the customers on the spot, as the platters were presented. We serviced hotels in Mumbai, Delhi, Kolkata, Bangalore, Chennai, Hyderabad, Pune, Rajasthan, Agra, Darjeeling, and Goa. Him-Icon's refrigerated trucks covered these routes daily, delivering cheese back and forth, filling the cold storage of our awaiting clientele.

Retail was also on my mind. Although retail in India had been moving from a largely bazaar approach to a more organized supermarket style, the vast majority of grocery shopping still occurred in bazaars. These bazaars held enormous charm and appeal for me, personally, but it certainly did not make it easy for us to get cheese into the hands of the Indian middle class. From April through September, the bazaars were sweltering. Women squatted over their spread of fresh cauliflower, spinach, radishes, and gourds, fanning themselves with their blue-orange-red saris. Imagine gourmet cheese in this setting!

So, in 2012, with guests at the hotels we had partnered with asking where they could buy the cheese they so enjoyed, we decided to launch our own Cowherd Creamery retail stores. Over the next two years, we systematically opened stores in eight major metros, attaining good coverage in each market with a chain of 80 stores. We positioned the brand as somewhat exclusive and high-end from a pricing standpoint, although not outrageously so, assuring the middle class plenty of access.

In parallel, we built our supplier network by recruiting franchisees who built up cheese-making expertise and capacity in villages all across India. We created an intensive training program for these franchisees, and we monitored them closely, practicing quality control and continued education on a systematic basis. We also had to help them create and maintain near-perfect sanitary conditions, in itself a major challenge. But the most crucial aspect was to teach the franchisees the difference between good cheese and great cheese.

As our budding artisan cheesemakers mastered this new vocabulary, developing mature palates able to appreciate the subtleties of each different cheese, the scalability of our venture started to appear viable. The entire operation was quite complex and challenging to put together, but the positive effect was that we had minimum competition. For outside of our experts there was little knowledge of the gourmet cheese-making process in India. And even for those who knew, they could not orchestrate the many pieces of our symphony of cheeses.

One of those myriad pieces was creative financing. By the time we got to the Cowherd Creamery venture, we had built a number of key relationships in the development finance world, as well as access to government financing schemes of various kinds. All of this came in handy since we had to guarantee loans for the cheese-making franchisees, as well as finance the real estate for our retail stores. It was no small puzzle, but once complete, the picture was beautiful – and quickly scaling.

We were able to add franchisees at a steady clip over the years, which drove our production capacity significantly. This generated capacity for us to enter the export market, catering especially to the rest of southern Asia and Southeast Asia.

By 2016, the Cowherd Creamery brand was an uncontestable phenomenon. Not since Amul launched its dairy cooperative in India in 1946 had a new dairy product brand generated so much excitement. Sixty some years later, our delightfully different business model, the Cowherd Creamery, boasts 100,000 cheese-making franchisees and 500 retail stores. And the Indian consumer's palate has been forever morphed to crave a touch of good cheese – at breakfast or with a glass of wine at Torquato Tasso.

HEALTHCARE

HARVARD MEDICAL SCHOOL, INDIA

As our MIT India project came into its stride, and MIT won tremendous international acclaim for vision and leadership in promoting open education, the folks at Harvard began to feel a little left out in the rain. They wanted their own high-profile cause to contribute to – and show off!

Thankfully, the opportunities to contribute were abundant. Especially in the domain of medicine and healthcare, India was floundering, unable to care for the vast population. India needed more doctors, nurses, medical assistants, and pharmacists. India needed a health insurance system that could cover the poor and the remote. India needed, overall, a fully thought-through healthcare system that could address its heartland and its downtrodden.

Two key questions emerged: (a) Where would we get the doctors, and (b) how would the rural Indian population afford their services? The doctors came from a medical education franchise à la MIT India. Similar to our strategy of partnering with MIT to offer engineering education, in this case we struck up a partnership with Harvard Medical School to train a large number of doctors. The second question, affordability, was addressed via an innovative medical insurance company, founded in 2009, which worked closely with the Indian government.

Two others ventures, Doctor at Hand, a rural pharmacy franchise, and Doctor on Wire, a small-town hospital and telemedicine franchise, were also formulated to address the full spectrum of gaps at the base of the Indian healthcare pyramid. First though: the Harvard Medical School project.

In February 2007, on the heels of a controversy over whether women had the intrinsic aptitude for science and engineering, stemming from comments made by previous president Larry Summers, Drew Gilpin Faust became the president of Harvard. Dr. Faust and Dr. Susan Hockfield, president of MIT since 2004, knew each other well. As we worked on the MIT India project, I started informing Dr. Hockfield about my burgeoning ideas on healthcare in India, including the need for an alliance with a top-ranking medical school. Dr. Hockfield mentioned the opportunity to Dr. Faust, following which, through a series of discussions, the idea of Harvard Medical School India gained form.

In 2010, Harvard Medical School, with its vast resources, became our partner, contributing a breadth of educational content that ranged from simulations to 3-D models, films, lecture videos, virtual reality renditions, and other immersive presentations on everything from heart surgery to cancer cell mutation.

Our two Indian partners in the project were, of course, Doctor at Hand and Doctor on Wire. To train our students, we licensed and utilized the incredible knowledge base created by Doctor at Hand. On their mobile phones, our students had access to the same content available to Doctor at Hand pharmacists. Through online role-playing games, the program called upon them to utilize that reference material and remedy specific situations and illnesses.

During the first two years of their training, students were assigned to a village to shadow a pharmacist at a Doctor at Hand pharmacy for three months each year. Students arriving at a village were immediately assaulted by diseases like malaria, asthma, and jaundice. And no longer in game-playing mode, they would have to come up with on-the-spot treatments in collaboration with the pharmacists.

They spent their remaining time during those first two years learning theory in a classroom setting, using the superb Harvard content. Some of the curriculum was structured as monitored self-learning, some as distance learning, and some as in-class instruction.

Doctor on Wire, on the other hand, became our training hospitals, with the 20 doctors at each Doctor on Wire hub supporting the hands-on education of 100 students. From years three to five, students shadowed a doctor, developing their specialization, and often a keen interest in the local population. So keen that many of our students stayed on to help scale Doctor on Wire. Starting in 2012, every hub produced 100 doctors per year – enough to support five new hubs.

Who paid for the education of these young doctors? Well, we developed an excellent education-finance scheme with HSBC that provided student loans on attractive terms. The loan repayment scheme was also set up directly with Doctor on Wire, such that as each student joined as an employee, they were automatically enrolled in a 10-year repayment program. There were also a series of foundation grants and fellowships. The Gates Foundation, dedicated to improving the state of global healthcare, endowed a major grant to finance the education of 100,000 students. Pharmaceutical companies like Ranbaxy and Merck also gave grants to support an average of 10,000 students per year. Our target number for 2020, however, was to train 600,000 doctors to staff 30,000 Doctor on Wire hubs.

We did an excellent job tackling heart and lung problems, eye and ear issues, and reproductive and pediatric health problems. By 2020, we managed to train 50,000 cardiologists, 100,000 pediatricians, 120,000 gynecologists, 150,000 ophthalmologists, 60,000 ENT specialists, 30,000 dentists, and 30,000 urologists. A fine team to begin the massive undertaking of healing Indian healthcare, but definitely only the beginning.

Cancer and neurology were harder to address. There were a limited number of doctors trained in cancer treatment, and those who were, were making such astronomical amounts of money that it was near impossible to attract them to such remote locations. However, in 2012, all this changed. A wonderful white-haired gentleman – an oncologist from Massachusetts General Hospital in Boston – came to us with a proposal. Dr. Wilson offered to quit Mass General and run a cancer-training program for us. His only condition: that we set up his facility in the heart of the Himalayas.

We established Dr. Wilson's training center in a small town in Sikkim, not far from the Pemayangtse monastery, deep in the magnificent panorama of the majestic Kanchenjunga Range. As the glass structure of the medical school rose like a phoenix out of our collective imagination, Dr. Wilson gathered a group of our top third-year students under Buddhist prayer flags flapping in the mountain wind. Here was our future; here were our soon-to-be cancer-ready Doctor on Wire hubs. And here also was an incentive we hadn't previously thought of: that advanced training centers in attractive spots helped us recruit international faculty.

In 2020, we have similar centers for cardiac surgery in Almora, and neurology in Dharamsala. And all told, we have trained 600,000 doctors while building a profitable, sustainable medical education system for India – our gift, Harvard's pride.

DOCTOR AT HAND

Many of my readers write to me with ideas for ventures. One, Dr. Vaman Shanbhag, a neurologist in Mumbai, sent me such an idea in 2008: "Just the other day I read an article in *DNA India* by you, and I was thrilled. I closed my eyes and thought of a future, and I think the health industry will change drastically from the way we see it today. The way mobile phones and PDAs are being used today, I feel that they will become an integral part of human existence, health, and life. What might come into existence in the future may be called Hand Held Health Devices." It was this letter of Dr. Shanbhag's that inspired Doctor at Hand.

The core idea behind our venture, founded in 2009, was that the Web held a tremendous amount of medical information and content covering common illnesses and their remedies, as well as relevant drugs, dosages, and other details of administering medication/treatment. But this repository of knowledge was scattered and not adequately searchable, such that medical professionals in remote parts of the world could properly utilize it. What if we organized this loose content and made it available through handheld devices?

At the back of my mind were my mother, my maternal grandfather, and one of my aunts, none of whom were trained in medicine, but each, through experience and interest, had developed abilities to administer medication for common ailments. My aunt specialized in homeopathy, my grandfather in allopathic medicine, while my mother had knowledge of both. They were treating members of the family, friends, and household staff for stomachaches, diarrhea, flu, headaches, and myriad other small discomforts. It seemed to me that they had enough intelligence and interest to do more if they had access to reference manuals, along with a bit more training. It was this access and training that we wanted to provide through Doctor at Hand.

It was critical to gather a simple, wizard-based user interface, accessible by cell phone, so to deliver this repository to the fingertips of millions of users. So, at the beginning of our journey, we set out to create a searchable knowledge base of this content. This knowledge base also made it possible to draw up an analysis of the key drugs needed to stock a small pharmacy.

Our value proposition to pharmaceutical companies: we would create a franchise of pharmacies throughout the heartland of India to both stock their products and administer treatment. For in many of these remote villages, there were no doctors, no hospitals, no remedy.

Here we would train pharmacists and arm them with the cell phone–based support, with which, for 80% of common illnesses, they could administer treatment. Our value proposition also included creating and managing the supply chain of drugs to these remote pharmacies, updating our knowledge base to roll out new drugs as they developed and making sure our pharmacists were well trained in administration.

I first brought our idea to Mr. Atul Sobti, then CEO of Ranbaxy. He listened with interest, probing where he was unclear. Then, at the end of my presentation, he smiled. "You have come up with an IT-based solution to India's colossal healthcare problem. It's quite brilliant."

Of course, the commercial implications for the drug companies were not lost on him either. It offered them a dramatically larger reach, expanding their addressable market exponentially. While the total available consumer market in India was large, the addressable market had been a huge problem due to lack of medical professionals in rural India. Who would diagnose the illnesses? Who would prescribe the drugs?

To scale our venture, we raised $30 million in three rounds of financing between 2011 and 2015 from a mix of drug companies and venture capitalists. We set up the Doctor at Hand pharmacies as franchises, partnering with several microfinance institutions (MFIs) to arrange financing for our franchisees in various villages. We partnered with Bioscope, the cinema company that had spread through rural India, to spread awareness about this franchise opportunity and recruit entrepreneurs. Each Bioscope cinema was armed with franchise applications to accompany the infomercials explaining the Doctor at Hand concept. Our ramp strategy closely mirrored that of Bioscope, and we joined them, tapping into their client base in nearly every village they entered. By 2020, this Bioscope marketing partnership introduced us to over 300,000 villages.

For the supply chain, we added an additional layer of creativity. While we had greatly penetrated the villages, we needed a hub-and-spoke distribution channel to pick up inventory from distribution hubs of pharmaceutical companies and deliver them along the last miles of more remote areas. For this, we used the micro-franchise model once again, training a new category of micro-entrepreneurs. These entrepreneurs quickly fulfilled our delivery service needs, shuttling between their village and the closest distribution hub. A lone driver bumped out over rutted roads with a truck full of insulin pumps, delivering a cure for diabetes to those who had thus far assumed that God, rather than medical devices, held the key to their health.

With the franchise marketing and delivery chain in place, the remaining piece of the puzzle was training. Here, once again, Bioscope proved to be a great partner. We leased their facility for six months of morning sessions to deliver distance-learning programs to train 35 pharmacists per village. After launch, we continued training sessions once a week to keep pharmacists abreast of professional developments. Then, once a month, we also sent a doctor to each village to answer questions and help diagnose unresolved cases, many of which fell naturally outside the realm of the pharmacists' expertise.

Part of our intent was to create redundancy as well as reach. While the pharmacy trained 35 people at once, it only employed the top 10 on-site. The other 25 were given the opportunity to buy a cell phone and build a private practice based on house calls. Again, this third genre of entrepreneurs was also financed by our deep group of MFIs. And, branding-wise, they were Doctor at Hand–certified and had been given the specific charter of prevention-oriented treatment, including vaccinations, which gave them credibility with outlying clientele.

With this three-pronged micro-franchise model, we found ourselves guaranteeing a lot of credit. Maybe too much, if we had not had a plan of action. But we mitigated the risk profile of our venture by limiting our exposure to a limited set of loans, while introducing a World Bank Guarantee beyond our acceptable threshold. The World Bank Guarantee (WBG) was a new class of financial service that we, along with a group of MFIs and micro-franchise companies, helped bring to market. Designed to offer incentives to scaling micro-franchise enterprises, the WBG has had enormous impact in alleviating poverty across the world by offering the foundation upon which hundreds of thousands of small entrepreneurs have built their viability.

In 2020, Doctor at Hand serves 300 million people, attending to their day-to-day medical needs so they can attend to their own day-to-day *wants*.

DOCTOR ON WIRE

With Doctor at Hand, we had set out to build a network of pharmacies addressing the common illnesses that spread annually across rural India. While such common illnesses could be tackled without trained doctors, there remained a tremendous, and yet unanswered, need for actual doctors capable of diagnosing and treating more complex ailments in the far-reaching rural provinces. Doctor on Wire was our tele-medicine answer to this demand.

The concept was centered around local diagnostic clinics that ran a battery of symptom-based and preventive care–oriented tests. For example, those above age 45 were required to do blood tests every three months to check cholesterol, blood pressure, blood sugar, and other blood chemistry parameters. Similar to Doctor at Hand, we made available a medical knowledge base, accessible by mobile phone, to clinical nurses working on a case-by-case basis.

The diagnostic clinics were Doctor on Wire franchises equipped with medical equipment ranging from basic blood pressure monitors to X-ray and ultrasound machines, ophthalmoscopes, and so on. All the equipment necessary to sustain the health of the living, and bring into the world those awaiting their introduction.

We used a similar strategy as Doctor at Hand to finance the venture. GE Capital was a natural match. As one of the world's largest medical diagnostic equipment producers, GE had long realized the need for their products in India, but they had never been able to access the millions of waiting customers due to the absence of a viable business framework.

We also employed the micro-franchise formula to build a chain of entrepreneurs who owned and ran the clinics. With this opportunity to own a business, we had no trouble attracting competent people to move to remote geographies. The financing requirements were significantly higher in the case of clinics than pharmacies. Diagnostic equipment was expensive. Therefore, we downsized to one clinic for every ten villages. And of course, the World Bank Guarantee (WBG) came in handy with this greater financing need, making credit more easily deliverable to each entrepreneur.

In 2013, we opened our 150th Doctor on Wire clinic in the town of Mao, Manipur, at the border of Nagaland. The town is known for the colorful Mao-Naga dance, a tribal spectacle, which was the centerpiece of our opening ceremony. Inside the clinic, expert technicians from GE trained the clinic owners and staff on how to operate cutting-edge magnetic resonance imaging technology. Outside, the Mao-Naga dancers rehearsed their chants. The lush surrounding hills looked on in amusement.

Every clinic was linked via high-bandwidth connectivity to a regional hub hospital where a team of doctors was stationed. This team of doctors owned and operated their own franchises, for which we also arranged financing through our partner banks. Each hub supported 10 clinics, or 100 villages. We started operating with 20 doctors per hub, with different specializations, all together supporting a territory of 100,000 people. Over time, we were able to scale the number of doctors per hub, such that the ratio of doctors to patients improved from 1:5,000 to 1:2,000.

Five years into the project, our coverage was shadowing Doctor at Hand, whom we distributed medication through. Our doctors also held local chambers at Doctor at Hand facilities on a monthly basis. On the day of the chamber, long, serpentine lines grew outside the pharmacy; the ailing and the elderly were brought in on rickshaws; women arrived with babies on their hips until, in line, they squatted to fan themselves and their children with the ends of their saris; grateful patients came with offerings of green papayas or coconuts. Patiently, the doctor in charge attended to each and every case.

Surgery, needless to say, had to be done at the hubs. For the first five years, we partnered with the closest existing hospital to each hub. This was not easy to scale, and very often we were faced with inadequate infrastructure. The lack of facilities and doctors in the heartland of India was an acute problem. We knew that eventually we would have to start layering on our own offering. Eventually, in 2015, we attached regional nursing homes, which included full operating capacity, to our hubs.

Today, we have a thriving network of Doctor on Wire centers stretching from Mizoram to Kachchh, from Kashmir to Kanyakumari. Clinic staff buzz in and out recording cardiac X-rays, screening mammograms, and sending them across the wire before advising patients on next steps – their calm confidence and unshakable commitment a testimony to the culture we have created in our franchises.

This confidence, of course, comes straight from the phenomenal range of services we have made accessible. A shopkeeper in Madhavpur can access angioplasty; a Sherpa in Gezing can get a much-needed colonoscopy; women once abused by their mothers-in-law for their inability to conceive can now get myomectomies to remove uterine fibroid and other obstacles to conception. Through the length and breadth of India, a revolution has taken place, altering the population's approach to life and death. Prayers are now aided by visits to Doctor at Hand pharmacies and Doctor on Wire clinics, where the questions of life and death are rightly answered.

DOCTOR FOR SURE

One of the most contentious topics in the 2008 US presidential elections was healthcare policy, which Barack Obama, the landslide victor, pushed aggressively towards universal coverage. As I delved into the topic from the perspective of India, hoping to outline a business plan for a sustainable, for-profit venture – not a nonprofit or a government agency – Doctor for Sure emerged.

Doctor for Sure is a medical insurance provider that makes healthcare available for a much larger population than was previously possible. We have been working closely with Doctor at Hand and Doctor on Wire, and we share certain common philosophies. Most important of which is that prevention is better than cure. As a result, we created a primary care program for all our clients in which they are consistently checked, tested, and treated with preventive care.

In order to achieve this, we maintain a comprehensive database of all our clients and their health-related information. These records are shared with both our partners, Doctor at Hand and Doctor on Wire, and with the Gates Foundation.

By the time Bill Gates retired from Microsoft to go full-time with the foundation, the Bill and Melinda Gates Foundation had already come to the conclusion that vaccines were among the most effective health interventions. By 2009, more than 100 million children were immunized annually against tuberculosis, polio, measles, and other diseases. But millions of other children, mostly in the world's poorest countries, were not immunized. The Gateses saw this as a relatively low-hanging fruit to address.

We approached the Gates Foundation with our plans for our four-pronged strategy of medical education, insurance, distributed pharmacies, and hospitals, and we proposed to take on the delivery aspect of their vaccination charter through Doctor at Hand pharmacies. The foundation, however, would be working with the insurance company, Doctor for Sure, to finance the vaccines.

The Gates Foundation was having success funding research in the domain of vaccination, but the last mile of delivery to the children was proving cumbersome. NGOs were their primary vehicle, but this was neither an effective channel, nor one that satisfied Mr. Gates. Its scaling capacity was too small, and its inability to address the operational complexity too great.

Bill was looking at the statistics: "Every year, 2.4 million children die from preventable diseases despite the availability of effective vaccines. Millions more survive, but they're left severely impaired. The long-range effects of childhood illnesses hinder the ability of those who survive to become educated, work, or care for themselves or others. This puts a strain on their families and on the economies of developing countries."

And he was looking at the operational complexity: "Successfully delivering high-quality vaccines requires a comprehensive temperature-controlled delivery system called the 'cold chain.' Vaccines need to be transported at the correct temperature to prevent them from either freezing or being exposed to too much heat. But in many countries, it's difficult to ensure this type of transport from the airport to the children in the village who need the vaccines."

Thus, our proposal to administer the vaccination of Indian children was an answer to Bill Gates's prayers. He felt that his goal "to increase the use of effective but underused vaccines and introduce new vaccines to prevent a total of four million deaths per year" had a chance of success with a three-way partnership with Doctor for Sure and Doctor at Hand.

One of the places where I found we could make advances surpassing the US healthcare system was in the staggering administrative costs. In 2007, the US spent $2.26 trillion on healthcare, or $7,439 per person – $1,000 of which was administrative costs alone. In 2007, out of a population of over 300 million, 45.7 million people in the US were uninsured, which leveled the administrative cost of the system at over $250 billion. This jaw-dropping number stared at me like a bottomless sewage pit of wasted resources.

From the outset, therefore, we worked to cut administrative costs by extensively using technology so that claims filing, processing, validating, and reimbursing were all low-overhead activities. For example, Doctor at Hand pharmacists would administer a vaccine and immediately log the procedure through their handheld into the main database. Validations were done through text messaging. And co-payments, as well as policy payments, were accepted through mobile phones. This enabled us to offer insurance policies to the base of the pyramid at remarkably low prices previously inconceivable.

With these steps – the extensive use of technology and the partnership with Gates – Doctor for Sure became an internationally watched venture. We published an article in the *Harvard Business Review* about our model. It offered a thorough analysis of the technologies we adopted and their impact in delivering a scalable, affordable healthcare system into the heartland of India. And as we started implementing the project, rolling out programs in village after village, we also published continuous reports on our corporate blog, which was syndicated by the *Times of India*. The blog offered ongoing reports on vaccination numbers, new technology introduction, and new drug and cure deployment and their success. It also offered perspective on breakthroughs in cost-optimization techniques that were closely watched by the British and the French, whose nationalized healthcare systems had brought their countries to their knees in terms of costs. The international healthcare community watched with wonder as we experimented and delivered a comprehensive private system without losing control of the cost equation.

A number of high-profile corporations started using our corporate program, including Maya Ray, NCTV, AdiShakti, Bioscope, Gangotri, Gagori, Camellia, Palanquin, and Urja. Their rural and small-town operations leveraged the healthcare infrastructure brought to market by Doctor at Hand, Doctor on Wire, and Doctor for Sure to deliver quality care in places that had never experienced modern medicine. In addition, we were providing corporate insurance for the entire manufacturing and mining sectors, also in relatively remote areas. In those geographies, often, we were by far the best as well as the cheapest option for the employers. In fact, it was by working closely with the corporations working in rural India that we managed to scale the three-part healthcare system that has today become India's pride in the international scene.

One of our greatest achievements was our work with Tata Steel. In many of the mineral-rich areas of India, corporations faced tribal conflicts around displacement issues. Yet globally, the mining industry was booming. World prices of minerals, ores, and metals had soared to record levels, a trend that began in 2002 with unprecedented demand from China. In 2006, global prices of all minerals skyrocketed up 48%.

In 2010, Jharkahnd's Tentoposi village was one such conflict-ridden place. Sitting on rich mineral reserves of iron ore, residents of this village were constantly under the fear of displacement and loss of livelihood sources.

Tata Steel had already announced that it would set up a 12-million-ton integrated steel plant in the area at an investment of Rs. 42,000 crores. The villagers suspected that there were people lurking around the village to usurp their land. Volunteers, wielding bows and arrows, guarded the barricaded village, and no government official or media person was allowed in.

Against this backdrop, Doctor for Sure became one of the key negotiating points in the steel company's negotiation with the tribal villagers. Tata offered them stellar medical care of the kind that they could not ever imagine, as well as guaranteed jobs and housing in the mines. We gave tours of Doctor at Hand and Doctor on Wire facilities elsewhere to the tribal leaders, and we explained the Doctor for Sure insurance program to them. It would not be an exaggeration to claim that it was this comprehensive healthcare incentive that finally turned the tide on Tata's negotiation. The case received extensive media coverage, establishing Doctor for Sure, Doctor on Wire, and Doctor at Hand as a required partner for all corporations venturing to work with tribal and rural populations.

As we scaled, farmers and many other small businesses bought their own insurance through us, and we also created a generous and welcoming individual coverage offering. Aside from these, we were the primary administrator of a number of government programs that insured the least privileged of the population.

Of course, the basic coverage for primary care was not adequate in many cases, and it would be a misrepresentation to say that we could bring universal healthcare of the highest quality to everyone in India. But we did succeed in offering primary care to almost 100 million previously uninsured patients, particularly in rural and small-town India where access to quality healthcare had been nonexistent.

We hope that, over time, we will be able to bring affordable healthcare to an even broader population, leaving no one uncared for. Meanwhile, we continue to press forward, and in 2020, we are a profitable $2 billion enterprise – giving us the wherewithal to take on more.

CARE

The number of millionaires rose faster in India than anywhere else in the world in 2007 – up 22.7% to 123,000 people. Today, in 2020, the number stands at an astonishing 1.23 million. It is this segment that we focused on for our venture, Care.

Simply put, Care was founded to offer a reliable, trained pool of in-home caregivers to address the needs of families with elderly, as well as patients with cancer, Parkinson's, Alzheimer's, stroke victims, or mental illnesses such as bipolar disorder, schizophrenia, depression, and myriad other illnesses that require some form of assisted living.

Some statistics would help us frame the problem. There were an estimated 2.5 million identified cases of cancer in India in 2007, let alone those that were not diagnosed. Mental illness was estimated to afflict 65 per 1,000 people, translating to nearly 70 million patients. However, there was only one trained psychiatrist for every 100,000 patients with mental illness. In addition, about 77 million elderly people needed to be looked after. All told, we were looking at a market of hundreds of millions of families that needed care.

Having experienced American society firsthand – an isolated, individualistic society, long on achievement, short on compassion – I believed that as India continued to develop, it would face certain choices about how to address the issue of caring for its non-producing citizens. It is a long, complex subject, and by no means did I have any illusion that Care could solve the entire problem. However, we felt that by training 100,000 women who were otherwise left out of the workforce to provide nursing and in-home care, we could achieve two things: (a) help a segment of the population with means to care for their in-need family members, and (b) train and create jobs for a large number of women who were otherwise unemployable.

In my parents' household in India, we employed a woman, Jaya Chatterji, to look after my grandmother. She was not educated; in fact, she could not even read or write. But she was kind and competent, had excellent eldercare training, was compatible with our family, and she quickly became a member of the household while caring for my grandmother through her advanced years. It was women like Jaya that I felt could become the cornerstone of Care, providing affluent Indian families high-quality care for their elderly, mentally ill, and otherwise afflicted family members.

In our hiring, we collaborated with the best NGOs in India, many of whom worked with abused and battered women, helping them leave their husbands and become self-sufficient. Our Care venture became one of the ways these women could find a livelihood and self-esteem through training and job placement. It was also important that these women were living at homes, where the dynamic of being part of a family was key to their rehabilitation.

Initially, we piloted the service with just 10 women from Maitreyi, an NGO in Mumbai, and trained them specifically in Alzheimer's care. We then placed a classified ad in the Mumbai edition of the *Times of India*, from which we received a few hundred queries from interested families looking for in-home, trained Alzheimer's care. The 10 women we had on hand were immediately scooped up – each with 20-plus offers to find within their preferred family situation. One of them, Asha Nagarkar, had a three-year-old daughter, who would, of course, need to move with her. Only three of the 20 families were open to this arrangement. So Asha chose a family in Andheri because they too had a daughter, Radha, around the same age, and the two girls first became playmates, then best friends.

It was a perfect win-win formula. And the families, as we explained our double–bottom line mission, understood that. As Asha and her nine colleagues found employment, we rapidly recruited another 100 women, training them in Alzheimer's care as well. By the end of 2010, we had 500 women placed in various affluent households in Mumbai, caring for Alzheimer's patients.

Gradually, we expanded the training to Parkinson's, bipolar disorder, schizophrenia, cancer, and other illnesses. And our NGO partnerships also expanded, alongside our advances into other Indian cities.

The stories of Asha and her colleagues spread quickly through NGO circles, and more and more women sought work with Care. The stories also became widely known in the affluent societies of major Indian cities. Asha's employers, Arun and Sudha Mehta, became great patrons of Care, and they helped us gain visibility out of pure goodwill.

Arun Mehta, in fact, ran a PR agency, and he knew numerous journalists in Mumbai. Soon, Asha Nagarkar of Care became a well-known name, representing the cause of Alzheimer's patients in India. We started getting phone calls from people looking for someone like Asha Nagarkar to care for their father, their mother, their aunt.

By 2020, our revenue stands at $1.65 billion, with a 20% operating margin. Not bad for being built on word of mouth, for being built on the recommendations of those families we've been fortunate enough to help. Together we've made Care an integral part of affluent India's formula for caregiving. And in doing so, we've placed more than 350,000 women, some with children, in families and homes where their skills were direly needed and openly appreciated.

LIFESTYLE BRANDS

URJA

For years, I had traversed India, wondering how to take advantage of the tremendous craftsmanship that existed in the far depths of India. In Nagaland and Gujarat, in Kashmir and Bengal, India's countryside has always been rich with artisans. Yet, for all its creativity, a certain sophistication of design and quality of finish remained elusive. Indian designs were always too complex, too busy. Thick gold threading. Heavy embroidery. The potential for a strong international fashion brand seemed somehow forever just out of India's reach.

Though the question appeared to me fully formed, the answer was years in the making, until one final explosive evening during a vacation in Italy in the spring of 2007. Dominique and I were staying with Carol and Ginou in the Tuscan village of San Giovanni d'Asso. India was far from my mind. In the distance, dusk was settling into vineyards, the rolling hills turning slowly from gold to black. That evening a friend of our host's, Alessandro, came for dinner. Alessandro had been a top executive at Giorgio Armani in Milan, and he had traveled widely in India.

The question I was asking had also been on his mind. "What would you name a fashion brand that is a blend of Italian design and Indian craft?" Alessandro asked as we sipped Carol's Avignonesi.

I had a name waiting, one that I had suggested for a friend's newborn daughter not long before. And that evening, under the Tuscan moon, Urja, which means "born out of creative energy," was conceived.

Over the next two years, we kicked around ideas, talked with people, and worked towards recruiting a core team to pilot our concept. Our core hypothesis: if Italian designers were made to work with Indian artisans, a new sophistication in design could be achieved.

We tested this with chikan, a style of embroidery common in Lucknow, as part of the pilot. Our Italian design team in Milan and our chikan team met in Lucknow. Walking through the bazaars, the Italians developed a sense of the craftsmanship that existed in the chikan industry. They took tens of thousands of photographs, bought samples, and soaked in the ambience while enjoying the biryani and kebabs. Then they spent three months in the design lab in Lucknow.

When the first set of renderings arrived, we were delighted to see that without losing the beauty, intricacy, and charm of the original art form, the Italians were able to achieve a previously unattained simplicity. There before us on the table lay a simple set of the most elegant Indian dress shirts.

The next two big issues were quality control and cut. Indian designers had very little experience in what I call "design for manufacturability," which is essential for a scalable ready-to-wear industry. While they had deep experience in designing salwar-kameez, ghagra-choli, and saris, they had little to none in Western clothing. The industry had to be trained in cut and manufacturing to spec. For this, we turned to Alessandro's contacts in the Italian fashion industry, recruiting a top-notch team of manufacturing experts.

With those three legs of our plan in place, and Alessandro's retirement all but scuttled, we raised money. Alessandro led the process, bringing to the table the top investors in the European fashion world. Europe, by then, had come to terms with the fact that the main consumer markets of the twenty-first-century were going to be India and China, and they saw Urja as an opportunity to invest in that future.

In July 2009, we met Patricia Barbizet, CEO of Financière Pinault and Artémis, a holding company with wide-ranging interests including Gucci, Balenciaga, Bottega Veneta, and Yves Saint Laurent. Over dinner in Paris, Alessandro explained our vision to her and showed her a portfolio of photographs. That night, we sealed the deal in principle, although much due diligence remained before the check came in.

We introduced the Urja brand first at Printemps in Paris, one of Artémis's key retail holdings. From there, we secured a space in Neiman Marcus in the US, and Takashimaya in Japan. In India, we sold through our own stores at high-end shopping malls and fashion streets. Today, we have flagship stores on the Champs-Élysées in Paris, Via Condotti in Rome, and Fifth Avenue in New York, among others. We also sell on the Web through our own personalized store, which has allowed us to build close customer relationships the world over.

The advantage to this close community is that we carefully monitor customer feedback, and in fact, we engage customers in online pre-design focus groups. Our designers learn so much through these interactions, and during pre-launch of new concepts, we return to this core customer base to check our assumptions.

One by one, we incorporated Bengali tassar silk, Rajasthani block printing techniques, Dhakai Jamdani fabrics, Gujarati mirror and bnadhni work, Kashmiri shawls, and even tribal artisans' work into our collections. We paid attention to every detail – from buttons to drawstrings – with artisans who created the most unique collections. And for this, our Italian-Indian fusion brand became a sensation, injecting a new aesthetic into a global fashion world that had, by and large, gone stale.

Urja, indeed, was born out of creative energy. However, the business was chiseled carefully, keeping in mind our core vision: simplicity, detail, sophistication, and quality. And with that, we seduced the fashion world.

OISHI

During the dot-com rush, two companies caught my eye: online diamond retailer Blue Nile, and online gift retailer RedEnvelope. Blue Nile had keyed in on a simple insight: the psychology of diamond shopping is informational as opposed to experiential. In other words, men attack the complex topic of diamond selection based on cut, color, clarity, carat, shape, and price. Not the blue Tiffany box. The company focused on the slightly awkward, often geeky demographic of male shoppers, and built a $300 million business, surviving the dot-com meltdown with a flourish.

In parallel, RedEnvelope zeroed in on the overly complex process of gift-giving. Mike Moritz, the legendary venture capitalist from Sequoia Capital, bought into the investment thesis of simplifying gift-giving via an online retail site. The company built a significant revenue stream, topping $100 million, before being run into the ground by poor management.

In 2006, I looked at RedEnvelope as a leverage buyout opportunity, but I found two problems: brand positioning and merchandising. In Oishi, we addressed both. Positioned as a high-end online gift retailer, Oishi offered a unique portfolio of merchandise catering to busy, professional, but still style- and taste-conscious, women. We served as personal shoppers for this demographic, saving one of their scarcest resources: time.

For our core audience, gift-giving occasions were many. There were the usual holidays, birthdays, weddings, anniversaries, plus the day-to-day occasions, such as a dinner party at a friend's house, to which people would normally bring wine, flowers, or chocolate. Our customers wanted to bring something different – something special. The Oishi Web site catalogued those whom customers purchased gifts for, as well as what they were gifted, making sure these special gifts were never repeated. It also featured a software personalization engine which tracked the tastes and preferences of (a) the women giving the gifts and (b) those receiving them.

Our merchandising had to align with the "special" feel we promised in the brand. To achieve that, we went back to certain core ideas we explored in Urja.

A long time ago, my father worked with the Ramakrishna Mission on a slum rehabilitation project in Kolkata called Rambagan. The members of this community had developed fine bamboo and cane products. However, as we experienced with the chikan artisans at the onset of Urja, they lacked in design and quality standards, keeping major markets out of their reach. Years later, at a gallery in Santa Fe, I happened upon some beautiful cane baskets and sculptures – this time by a Japanese artist – but at astronomical prices. I wondered if we could achieve the elegance and sophistication of the Japanese designs with our Indian artisans at a fifth or tenth of the prices before me.

I had been a fan of Japanese design and craftsmanship for as long as I could remember, so I connected these two data points and hired a design team from Japan to work with artisan communities in India. The resulting high-quality, masterfully designed gift products ranged from bamboo to woodwork, textiles to ceramics, jewelry to paper.

Japanese designers were paired with sandalwood artisans in South India, textile artisans in Gujarat, jewelry artisans in

Rajasthan, paper artisans in Pondicherry, seashell artisans in Orissa, and candle artisans in Kolkata. Products included marvelous scarves, table linens, cushion covers, baskets, jewelry boxes, jewelry, candles, incense, oil lamps, photo albums, writing journals, shawls, kaftans, sleepwear, sculptures, and artifacts. Even our packaging was exquisite, drawn from the work of our thriving paper artisans. And with these offerings and price points between $20 and $200, our average gross margin exceeded 67%.

One final piece of financial engineering gave us excellent leverage. We structured deals with several of India's top microfinance institutions – Bandhan, SEWA Bank, SKS – such that they were willing to lend money to our artisans as long as we served as a marketing channel for their products. Of course, we were happy to provide such a guarantee as long as the artisans agreed to work with our designers, producing merchandise that would sell to a sophisticated American audience.

In November 2014, like every year, we went for Thanksgiving with our friends, the Cooksons, in Hillsborough. As soon as I walked into Margot Cookson's arms, she whispered into my ear, "I have to show you what Anne got me!"

In a splash of handmade turquoise paper, a box lay open on the table. An exquisite bamboo sculpture sat in it. "It's a lampshade," I said, recognizing the design.

"Oh?" Margot said. "I thought it was a sculpture!"

"It's both," boomed Margot's daughter Anne from behind us, enjoying the sensation her gift had caused.

Margot took me aside later in the evening and whispered again, "I feel terrible. Anne spent so much money on me." Now, this put me in an awkward position. The lamp, I knew, cost $150. I was sure Margot thought it cost 10 times as much, and she was going to look for ways of giving something of equivalent value to Anne on the next occasion. Yet, I didn't want to spoil Anne's glee. Before I left that night, I said to Margot, "Look up Oishi.com tomorrow." We had tens of thousands of such delighted customers.

With each customer averaging 20 transactions per year, at a $40 average transaction size, our total annual business volume per customer was $800. Within five years, we grew to $250 million. And in 2020, Oishi is a billion-dollar enterprise. And with broadened segments and international suppliers, we have repeated the same supply-chain model in Africa, Latin America, and Southeast Asia. Land RedEnvelope had only dreamt of.

THAKUR

In June 2008, I was in Kolkata for my aunt's funeral. As ever, our very large Elgin Road extended family congregated over several meals. As the morning kirtan ended, tables and chairs were briskly arranged to serve lunch in the lawn tent. After lunch, chairs were shuffled again for a session of Rabindrasangeet. Then rearranged again for dinner. Another big lunch the following day to end the 10-day mourning. Whether for a birth or death, no matter the reason for our coming together, these meals always acted as catalyst for bonding, and they held for us a place of supreme importance.

The meals were cooked by an Oriya chef, Shankar Thakur, who had first come to our family some 40 years ago from his village, Manglojodi. He had witnessed the rearing of many children, cooked meals for puja after puja, and mourned with us the many deaths. The kitchen had changed over those years. The family fractured. Microwaves and gas ovens replaced coal fires. But he remained our family cook through all those years, only leaving in the end to develop his own catering practice. He started cooking for the Saha Institute of Nuclear Physics, where my aunt taught. He catered weddings and naming ceremonies. And on these major occasions, he always returned to shower us with his lavish culinary talents. With dhnoka and chhanar dalna, with chholar dal and payesh, his cuisine brought back memories of a lost time.

As I watched Shankar Thakur serve plate after plate of shukto, polao, pnathar mangsho, and chandan khir, I could not help but think about the dreadful packaged food products that littered the shelves of American grocery stores. My entrepreneur mind had always wondered why the great cuisines of the world were not marketed as packaged food in the same way that, say, Campbell's soup was.

Just to give some context, the Campbell Soup Company manufactures soups, beverages, confectionery, and prepared food products. In 2008, the company passed 136 years of age, with over $7 billion in annual sales and a portfolio of more than 20 market-leading brands – including Campbell's soups, Swanson Broths, Pepperidge Farm cookies, Pace Mexican sauces, Prego pasta sauces, Godiva chocolates, and Arnott's biscuits of Australia. It had even acquired the Wolfgang Puck soup business from Country Gourmet Foods – a line of products that was actually quite tasty.

Campbell had also announced its plans to expand into emerging markets, starting with China and Russia. Could India be far behind? In 2007, the Indian packaged food industry grew 15% – a jump that surely registered on Campbell's radar. Clearly, packaged food was an enormous market opportunity globally, and a market in which India should have been playing a more significant role. But it wasn't. Not in 2008. This was the backdrop of our venture, Thakur.

With this company, we wanted to tackle a few key opportunities. First, the market for good quality packaged food was global and underserved. I had a fair bit of exposure to dual-career middle-class families in the US who struggled to put hot food on the table for dinner. Careers had taken over. Junk food had swamped the market. Obesity was a national problem, and it was quickly ballooning into a global one. The need remained focused on ready-to-eat, but now the market was demanding something more – *healthy*.

Second, packaged food still suffered from the problem of taste degradation, unless it was frozen. Frozen food, however, had limited shelf space, was difficult and expensive to transport, and was, overall, not the most promising segment to go after.

The challenge this analysis posed was that we needed food processing technology that could preserve food for extended shelf life, without any taste degradation. So, at the genesis of our venture, we focused on acquiring this technology. We collaborated with Cornell University's Institute of Food Science and Technology on primary research in flavor preservation. We recruited a team of chemists in our lab in India, who worked closely with the Thakur-funded Cornell team.

It was not at all clear after six months that the team would be able to deliver. The two teams argued endlessly about the approach to solving the problem in hand. I knew nothing at all about chemistry, and I did not have a clue as to how to resolve the conflict. In March 2009, I facilitated an off-site meeting with the two teams in Cornell. We invited five different objective experts in the field to attend the off-site as paid consultants. At the end of this combative, often belligerent three-day off-site, we concluded that the Indian team's approach happened to be better – not an easy pill for the Cornell team to swallow. My goal, however, was not to fire the Cornell team. I wanted them on the project, and I negotiated hard to resolve the ill will so we could move forward.

With leadership now in place, the next six months were more productive. In 2010, after 18 months of intense stress, we had the technology. And in 2011, we launched our first line of delicious, reasonably priced, healthy packaged food products in collaboration with Tesco, the UK's premier grocery retailer. Tesco was already working on entering the US market at the time, and we invited them to invest in Thakur. In effect, we became Tesco's private label packaged food brand, which gave us access not only to their UK stores, but also the fledgling US stores. From Sacramento to Zurich, chhanar dalna and kasha mangsho were being served nightly, steering families away from the treacherous McDonald's hamburger.

In 2014, after the Thakur brand gained market acceptance, we launched a lineup of Chinese cuisine. The recipes of the Chinese products came from cooks we hired from Tangra, Kolkata's Chinatown. It was a cuisine that I loved, but of which the world knew nothing. We introduced the Tangra brand through Trader Joe's in the US, who, by this time, was also carrying the Thakur products.

In parallel, we did a PR campaign with mommy bloggers, introducing them to the Tangra lineup. *Busy Mom* wrote, "Last night, my kids congratulated me on my newly acquired Chinese culinary skills. They polished off every last morsel of what I had placed on the table, and asked for more. Well, I didn't have more. Friends, busy moms, here's my secret…I did not cook this meal. I served it out of a Tangra packet from Trader Joe's."

In 2016, we launched similar product lines based on Italian, French, Thai, and Vietnamese cuisines. For French cuisine, we turned to the bistro style, creating a line of products including coq au vin, boeuf bourguignon, and cassoulet. We also included Belgian bistro dishes like waterzooi.

Our factories dotted the countryside of Orissa, taking advantage of the low cost of labor and the innate culinary culture. We hired chefs from Italy, France, Thailand, and Vietnam, who trained the Indian teams, led them through the processes, and with some of them, created entirely new fusion lines.

All told, we built a $7 billion global enterprise. And what took Campbell 136 years to do, we did in a decade. Our products spread across the world's table where families, even in these hectic times, are seated, passing each other their plates, the salt, the pepper – bonding.

DARJEELING

Our family has long been a connoisseur of Darjeeling tea. Growing up in Bengal, it is hard not to be. My great-aunt, in particular, brewed tea with a precision that I have rarely experienced elsewhere. My mother and my uncles each had their "sources" – tea merchants in Jagu Bazaar, Lake Market, New Market. Long before Dolly's Tea Shop became a Kolkata institution, they knew how to find the finest teas.

Years later, when I relocated to San Francisco, I plunged headlong into the cult of wine in the Napa Valley and the surrounding wine country. One September, I even worked on a vineyard in Oregon, pruning grapes, while visiting my friend, Dave Chen, whose Patton Valley Vineyard produced a fine pinot noir. As a Bengali and an entrepreneur, I could not help but ask the question: Why is India incapable of marketing tea the way wine is marketed by California, Oregon, Australia, New Zealand, and of course, France and Italy?

It was in January 2006, while staying on the Glenburn Tea Estate, that my thoughts on how to market Darjeeling tea started to coalesce. Nestled in layers of Himalayan ranges rising against the sky, upon abundant rolling hills of lush tea gardens, Glenburn was situated in an idyllic spot. We arrived by car on a winter afternoon and were greeted by Mrs. Neena Pradhan, our hostess. The bungalow was a beautifully restored English house with four suites, ours the Rose Suite. We had gone back it seemed a hundred years, to the times of the Raj.

After a lavish lunch, we walked down to a neighboring village. Prakash, one of the bungalow bearers, was our guide. At the end of the walk, he poured fresh lemonade into sunlit glasses on a tray with a tray-cloth. We sat at the edge of a mountain, sipping the juice, as Prakash smilingly asked us to guess what else he had put in the drink! We failed, of course. "An ever-so-slight touch of mint and ginger," he laughed. Personalized touches such as this were sprinkled throughout the experience, elegantly rendered and delivered with warmth and sincerity by the Glenburn staff.

Upon return to the bungalow, Neena had her afternoon tea ready. Delicious tea cakes and an outstanding autumn flush tea, made fresh from the latest harvest! The manager of the estate explained some of the details of the four flushes of tea. That tea grows nine months of the year, with the first flush harvested in February, followed by the second flush (stronger), the monsoon flush (lesser of the four flushes), and finally the autumn flush (a delightful mellow, but fragrant bouquet).

The next day, we went for another walk in the mountains. From the bungalow down to a campsite by the river Rungeet, we dropped from 3,300 feet to 800 feet – a beautiful, eight-kilometer downhill trek. The scenery was a gorgeous juxtaposition of the snow-capped Kanchenjunga Range and miles of lush tea plantations. All along, Prakash pointed out local vegetation, especially medicinal plants like jatamunsi, kutki, and so many others. At the lodge by the river, another lavish arrangement awaited us, deftly administered by four bearers. Drinks, barbecued appetizers, followed by a ten-course lunch at the river's edge.

Glenburn was a completely personalized experience, and shamelessly decadent. We loved it there and hoped more of the Darjeeling estates would build up similar destinations so the world could discover this Himalayan jewel in all its splendor.

So, when we started Darjeeling, our tea lounge venture, in 2009, the strategy had been steeping for several years. Central to the old dysfunctions of the tea market was the prevailing treatment of tea as a commodity, sold mainly in bulk. As a result, the warehouse brands like Lipton and Tetley bought in bulk and blended with lower grade produce to abide by a low price point, producing millions of bags of mediocre tea. In contrast, the top wines were the pride and joy of their makers, crafted with tremendous passion and patience. My thought was that if some of the 80-odd tea estates in Darjeeling were taught to produce their own hand-selected tea, crafted in a way akin to wine and marketed under their own private labels, Indian tea might not simply assume a place on the world market but lead it.

In 2010, therefore, we set up partnerships with 10 estates from which we would buy tea to sell to consumers, not as a commodity, but as a branded product. We also launched our tea lounge brand, Darjeeling, and modeled it after the Starbucks café concept. Starbucks was the world's largest coffee and coffeehouse chain with over 15,000 cafés in some 50 countries. However, unlike Starbucks, ours were elegant lounges, serving the choicest Darjeeling teas and a selection of delicate accompaniments in beautiful European porcelain tea sets.

We worked with our friends at Oishi to create the table linens for the tea lounges, and with some of the Thakur chefs to execute the delicacies. Nasturtium fritters, reminiscent of Glenburn, were accompanied by pumpkin flower fritters, an invention of my grandfather's. Samosas, empanadas, and momos mingled with scones and fish fingers, offering an international repertoire. Prawn cutlets, green pea kochuris, shammi kebabs, and ghugni flowed out of my mother's precise brain into the Thakur kitchens and, eventually, onto the Darjeeling tables.

We started with lounges in Mumbai, Delhi, Kolkata, Bangalore, Pune, Hyderabad, and Chennai. By 2012, lounges dotted each of those cities, as well as London, Paris, Rome, New York, Boston,

San Francisco, Los Angeles, Chicago, Seattle, and Barcelona. Three years later, we were deep into North America, Europe, China, Latin America, and, of course, India. We owned 40 of the 80 estates in Darjeeling. And we not only sold packaged tea through our lounges, but we also maintained a large market share at high-end grocery stores like Whole Foods and Trader Joe's.

We were marketing some 150 different labels of tea, and we had created an entire vocabulary around how to understand and appreciate tea – not only by taste, but also as a way of life. "Afternoon tea at Darjeeling," wrote the *New York Times*, "is the new way of doing business." Slow, refined, grounded in human relationships – that was the essence of the Darjeeling brand.

In 2018, we entered a new business, not so much for revenue or profitability reasons, but for branding. At each of our 40 estates in the Darjeeling Himalayas, we created five- to eight-room boutique hotels. If Glenburn had brought us this far, it was the least we could do to offer our customers a route back to such an experience – luxurious, splendidly beautiful, and steeped in a warm hospitality.

My dream, by 2020, had come true. Darjeeling, queen of the Himalayas, shone in full glory again, with the magnificent snow-capped Kanchenjunga Range smiling down on its own $4 billion enterprise, served cup after superb cup.

RENAISSANCE

For years, I had been disturbed by the demolition of India's architectural heritage. In the name of development, we have watched centuries-old homes leveled in a matter of hours, and in their stead multi-storied apartments climb oddly above the lilies of remaining rooftops. In Kolkata, I watched helplessly as British-era gems, old palaces, and homesteads disappeared one after another.

My family is old Kolkata. Our rice paddy fields greened as monsoons washed over them. Our heavy-limbed mango orchards bore the juiciest and most fragrant varietals. One of our vacation homes nestled in my grandfather's legendary rose garden in the now traumatized Bengal-Bihar border. Our relatives' houses dotted Kolkata. These old houses in the alleys of Pathuriaghata and Shyampukur were sprawling places, bearing the stories of Kolkata's now receding past. In the halls of the Ghosh family of Pathuriaghata, the All-Bengal Music Conference was founded in 1937, and Indian classical music, then a nascent art form, was nurtured under the patronage of Bhupendranath Ghosh. At the time, the mid-nineteen hundreds, only baijis (courtesans) sang publicly.

Manmathanath Ghosh was the first patron to invite Irabai Bardekar, a legendary musician, to the inner wing of his home, despite protests from his wife. He considered it his honor to host talent, and the legendary sitar maestro, Ravi Shankar, met his guru Alauddin Khan there. The family's drawing room once overflowed with music, food, hookah smoke, and attar fragrance, but in 2008 the front gate gaped open. A bony stray cow often wandered into the yard where the foyer's Belgian mirrors collected dust.

The past always recedes. Sensible people do not let that be bothersome. The old steps aside for the new, and so it should. Yet, looking out the car window driving through India, I was stricken by the pace and brutality of this transition. Chowringhee, Kolkata's once impressive Paris-esque boulevard, was layered in flyover roads obstructing views of British-era architectural gems such as the Indian Museum and the Geological Survey. The imposing Calcutta Club building had also lost its eminence with the intervention of the Lower Circular Road flyover. In South Kolkata, Sir Rajendranath Mookherji's house on 7 Harrington Street awaited its then unknown fate, a silent ponderer of its owners' declining prominence. The lure of escalating real estate prices would soon become too much. Sir B. C. Mitter's 19 Camac Street had already been demolished, a skyscraper in its place. The same for Raja Promotho Roy Chowdhury's 9 Hungerford Street overlooking the lake in Minto Park. In the older North Kolkata, Sir Kailash Bose's residence would soon be sold, wiping out another reel of childhood memories for my mother and grandmother. Ramdulal Sarkar's Beadon Street house, Digambar Mitra's Jhamapukur house, and Manmathanath Mitra's Shyampukur house were all still standing, but in dilapidated conditions; all of them, like elephants, would fold gently, horrendously, onto their knees.

As I was scouring for a business model with which to save these old houses that sat trembling under the dark eye of the cash-rich real estate developers, I received an e-mail from entrepreneur Hari Nair. Nair was then the CEO of HolidayIQ, an online travel company in India, studying the trends in the Indian tourism industry. One of the most interesting observations of the HolidayIQ data was that Indian travelers liked to travel in families and groups. They found that 22.14% of their audience traveled in groups of 3–5; 20.93% in groups of 6–10; and an overwhelming 40.43% traveled in groups larger than 10. A key driver for this last category was corporate groups, headed to off-sites and team-building experiences.

Another key data point in the study was that 56.62% of the travelers went for short, two- to four-day trips, while 35.84% went for one-day trips. Longer vacations were a luxury, available to a mere 7.54%. Not surprisingly, most of the shorter trips were intra-region, as the affluent urban middle class accessed quick holidays.

This data gave me the idea for our venture, Renaissance Holidays. The concept for Renaissance was to offer these expansive heritage properties as short, full-service vacation rentals. In other words, you could rent one of these houses for three to four nights, with a cook, maids, and nannies. Most of the houses had seven to ten rooms, perfect for both family vacations and corporate off-sites.

In addition, we added an extra layer of Renaissance thinking to the package. We created a network of artists, poets, musicians, and dancers with whom we held salons at each of our properties. Guests, thus, could have an eclectic, artistic experience fitted uniquely to their locale.

We scoured the red-soiled countryside of Birbhum and Purulia for the best Baul singers. In their saffron robes, ektara in hand, they sang, "Akhono to elona kaliya..." We invited qawwali groups from Pakistan. Doyens of Carnatic music graced the halls of Renaissance properties in Mysore and Madurai. Odissi dancers performed Jayadev's *Gita Govinda* in Puri. Kathak dancers twirled in the halls of a Lucknow palace, evoking Satyajit Ray's *Jalshaghar*.

We took our guests back in time.

In a Cooch Behar homestead, dinner crammed 20 around a table littered with round, puffy luchis, rich red goat curry, and an opulent choice of sandesh and rasogolla desserts. The children ate as fast as they could so to be excused, rushing back out into the ubiquitous smell of mangoes for intricate hide-and-seek games. They searched in the third-floor roof terrace and chased down the wrought iron spiral staircase that only the janitor was to use. They hid behind the shutters in the second-floor verandah, shrieked on the over-bridge that connected the main house to the outhouse, and were caught finally, gasping for breath in the greenhouse.

By 2012, we had acquired 200 such properties all over India. Not only did we acquire properties atop the Sahyadri hills and on the beaches of Gopalpur, but also along the narrow streets of Agra and Hyderabad. In Kolkata, for example, we acquired Sir Biren Mukherji's Camac Street residence, as well as Manmathanath Ghose's Pathuriaghata residence. While Sir Biren's was a British colonial mansion, the Pathuriaghata palace sprawled in classical Indian courtyard architecture. Each house had a history, a story, captured and told through our extensive Web site. By 2016, these stories relayed the past lives of 2,000 properties. And in 2020, we have 3,000 properties owned and operated by the Renaissance Holidays group.

When we started, we were charging an average of Rs. 20,000–30,000 ($400–$600) per night for an entire property, housing anywhere between 8 and 20 people, including food. Without much difficulty, we achieved 75% occupancy across our group. Prices have risen over our decade-long journey, and we have remained very profitable, doing close to $400 million in revenues. Also key in our business model is the fact that as India's real estate appreciates, so too do our properties. Our balance sheet, dotted with property and revenue, is incredibly impressive, offering a downright astronomical company valuation.

Today, our brand has become an international phenomenon. *Travel + Leisure* writes, "To experience the splendor of classical India, your trip must include a stay in one of the Renaissance properties. In quintessential style and unparalleled elegance, you will be drawn into the set of a period film, playing a role you could only dream of."

TILOTTAMA

In 1970, Shahnaz Husain single-handedly put Ayurvedic beauty products on the map when she founded her namesake herbal empire. From neighborhood beauty salons to retail stores to pharmacies, Shahnaz Husain–branded herbal products command a market coverage of unprecedented order. But in the 40 years that followed, no other major brand had emerged in what I saw as an expanding category of herbal beauty products.

The latter half of the 2000 decade saw a boom in the middle class's disposable income. Not only did this new money get spent on cafés and restaurants, or saris and kurtas, but on perfumes, cosmetics, and beauty products in a growing number of salons. It seemed the upwardly mobile female consumer market could easily support a new, differentiated herbal beauty brand – Tilottama.

According to Hindu mythology, Tilottama was an apsara – a celestial dancer, supple, gracious, poised, and elegant. "Tila" in Sanskrit means sesame seed, or tiny. "Uttama" means superior. Her name means, literally, a being whose tiniest particles are comprised of the finest of qualities. The apsara, Tilottama, was created by the divine innovator Vishwakarma, at Brahma's request, by assembling the best qualities of every being into one.

Our Tilottama line of beauty products was similarly differentiated at every step, from its packaging to its narrative. In branding we looked to one of my favorite examples: Chanel No. 5. Chanel arrives by way of a white box with a black border and simple black lettering. To me, that simple white box epitomized understated class. So, in a market rife with gaudy, unsophisticated designs, Tilottama's logo was a simple gold line drawing of a woman's silhouette against a black base.

Indians have always been obsessed with complexion, so any girl born dark faced a stigma. While in the educated urban classes the prejudice was slowly diminishing, the rural and underclass societies were still horrendously discriminating. Mothers of eligible sons refrained from arranging marriages with dark girls. A girl child born dark sent entire families into mourning. Even in the upper classes, darker girls spent countless morning hours in front of the mirror, wishing for some miracle to lighten their skin. And at night, they applied creams that promised such miracles. In fact, a $300 million fairness-cream market was growing at 20% per annum in 2010 because, predictably, the majority of Indian women were dark, a tropical sun bestowing them with its blessings.

This fair market, though growing, was not what Tilottama was after. For having lived in America for 20 years, I knew how the West craved a tan, how Anglo men were completely seduced by dark-skinned women. It was a simple matter of perceived value. In India the perception was flawed, generating in dark girls a self-esteem problem. After all, when society deems you inferior, when your parents mourn the color of your skin, how can a young girl get past all these painful scars? How can they not wish away the source of the scorn – their beautiful, glowing, albeit dark skin?

We decided to focus the entire Tilottama brand narrative on young, dark girls between 12 and 30 years of age. Above all else, we wanted Tilottama to give them self-esteem, confidence. To me, there was nothing more stylish than self-confidence, no attribute sexier than a razor-sharp mind.

Thus, the apsara Tilottama – the celestial dancer who could seduce any and all – took the form of a dark beauty. Our brand icon was a graceful, self-assured dancer with slender fingers and a confident, brilliant smile. We used striking images of her hands, her back, her neck, lips – abstract black and white photography along the lines of the nudes of California photographer William Carter.

However, we did not want to allow our differentiation to stop at the physical. The concept of beauty Tilottama embodied had an important three-dimensional characteristic, including the brain as one of the most important seductive features in a woman. Tilottama's brand narrative highlighted this element by including in the product line herbal oils that delivered both beautiful hair and an alert, sharpened brain.

We also differentiated on the production end. Our laboratory near Chennai recruited chemistry graduates from some of the top science colleges in India, including Presidency and Loyola, to work on advanced R&D. Here, we combined modern advances in chemistry with the ancient science of Ayurveda to deeply understand the impact of herbs on different types of human skin. The result was a series of distinct ideas based on basic Ayurvedic principles. For example, women all over India knew that applying a paste of turmeric to the skin before bed added a glow to their skin. But applying turmeric was messy. We created an easy-to-apply turmeric-based night cream, along with a chickpea-flour-based morning mask, which together gave the skin a thorough cleansing and highlighted the unmistakable glow.

Beyond this there was an array of ancient beauty tips that India's age-old wisdom had in store. A cucumber-based eye cream; a milk-curd-based body mask with rose water essence; and a lemon-based anti-dandruff oil just to name a few.

On the production side, today we have 30 Tilottama plants sprinkled throughout India, where our lipsticks and moisturizers, our essential oils and perfumes, are manufactured and packaged.

Thousands of rural people work diligently alongside our resident chemists, extracting, blending, and bottling products.

From these plants our products are then distributed through high-end retail stores at various malls, where we share shelf space with Estée Lauder and Christian Dior, our sophisticated packaging often outmatching theirs. And we have gone international, focusing on the Indian, Hispanic, African, and African American demographics. Herbal cosmetics for dark-skinned women was an international hole in the beauty business in 2008. Today we've plugged it and, in the process, built Tilottama into a global brand. So much so that while waiting for flights in London, San Francisco, or Singapore, I cannot help but notice in the duty-free shops the distinctive Tilottama portfolio. The elegant black box and gold silhouette. Our ancient celestial dancer is today a powerful modern icon of international femininity.

AMRAPALI

Amrapali is a world-renowned healing center franchise that has quickly rooted in the Indian countryside. Ensconced in betel nut groves, set amidst pristine green rice paddy fields, we built a chain of serene ashrams with rustic but well-equipped cottages, surrounding world-class massage facilities for those who desire more than the usual escape from their stressful lives.

The idea came to me while visiting Ubud, a village in Bali, where Dominique and I stayed at Waka di Ume, a small boutique hotel situated amidst the rice paddies. As I absorbed the beauty of the dark clouds reflected in the brimming paddies, it struck me that India had a gold mine to tap into. At Waka, and around the world, massage costs a premium. In Paris, an hour's massage could cost €130 ($182); in Tokyo, it could be 20,000 Japanese yen ($263); closer to home, at Palo Alto's Watercourse Way, an hour of deep tissue massage would set you back a minimum of $90. But in India, where labor costs were a fraction of Western costs, we identified the opportunity to train hundreds of masseurs in deep tissue massage, along with the Ayurvedic and aromatherapy forms, and deliver the service at an astonishing $10 an hour.

In 2010, Amrapali's first center, a 200-room terra cotta ashram, rose 100 kilometers outside Bishnupur amidst the rice fields of Bankura. The villagers had never seen construction of this scale. They watched for 18 months as the cottages gradually spread across their once empty land. Before long, it became the major employer for this region.

In conceptualizing the experience, I returned to a Zen monastery, Tassajara, that Dominique and I had experienced in California. In July 2005, we drove there through the winding roads deep into the Santa Lucia Mountains, wondering, often, whether we were lost. It seemed a never-ending journey to the end of the world. Tassajara was the first Zen monastery outside of Asia, founded by a Zen monk, Suzuki Roshi. Hidden away in a very remote part of Carmel Valley, it is encircled by high ridges and the deep Ventana wilderness. One particular memory I had of Tassajara was that at 5:20 each morning, a young monk ran through the dark of the place ringing a bell, breaking the sleeping silence. The guests would rise and dress, and soon appear in a slowly knotted group walking the moonlit paths back to the zendo for morning meditation. At Amrapali, I included this ritual of bell ringing before dawn to wake our guests for meditation.

Soon our all-inclusive six-day programs, ripe with twice-a-day massages, meditation sessions at dawn and dusk, yoga classes, sauna, swimming pools, and mineral baths, all woven within our delicious vegetarian cuisine, were gathering not only locals but a sweeping international clientele. The entire six-day program: $600 per couple.

We sprinkled Amrapali centers throughout Uttar Pradesh, Bihar, Orissa, Bengal, and Madhya Pradesh – India's major rice growing regions. There was something infinitely serene and earthy about the rice fields, how they swayed at dawn before harvest. Or in May, at dusk, how the dark clouds announced nor'wester storms. That became the essence of our brand. The tropical tranquility. The rhythm of the fields. The monsoon. The harvest.

The Amrapali staff was cloaked in light brown saris and sarongs. The cottages blended into the thatched huts of their surroundings, and they were decorated in the colors of hay, leaf green, and light buff. We offered white cotton kurtas and pajamas to the guests, and we asked that they wear them while in the ashram. It added a layer of simplicity and harmony to the place, and it helped the guests quiet the chatter of their otherwise busy minds.

By 2015, we'd built 18 centers and just over $100 million in revenue. Our annual occupancy hovered around 60%. April through June was sometimes hard to fill due to the heat, although the nor'westers in some of the centers held their own appeal. The monsoon was very popular, with the voluptuous rain, thunder, and lightning. Nature was alive, it evoked awe, reducing the dominance of the ego, an essential practice in Vedic spirituality.

Continued building approached on the horizon, and in 2020 we opened our one-hundredth ashram in a small village near Ujjain, in Madhya Pradesh. Amazing to think, standing in the isolated serenity of this most recent center, that across the country we have over 20,000 rooms, and we wake almost two million people annually, bell by bell.

Revenues from our six-day packages just crossed $1 billion. Occupancy is at 85%, and we now charge $750 per package – a price far below our international competitors, while more than adequate to employ each 200-person staff. All told we employ over 20,000 people, of whom almost 7,000 are trained massage therapists. Therapists for whom people travel from all over the world to lie under their masterly hands.

ENTERTAINMENT

ELIXAR

I have always been fascinated by Pixar. *The Incredibles* enthralled me. *Ratatouille* mesmerized me. And apparently I am not alone: The former, with a production budget of $92 million, grossed $631 million worldwide; the latter, with a production budget of $150 million, grossed $621 million. So much for cartoons as child's play.

The answer to how such numbers were reached boils down to enchanting characterization, tight, moving screenplays, superb graphics, and outstanding editing. It was only a matter of time before I started looking for ways to apply this formula to an India-based studio, working with Indian stories, colors, and culture. Disney had tried oriental stories earlier, with *Mulan* and *Aladdin.* However, the treatment in those movies remained distinctly American. I was after something much more Indian.

Now, to achieve the Pixar benchmarks in graphic excellence, we needed advanced technology combined with screenwriting and editing finesse. The latter two were relatively lower barriers to entry, skills abundantly available in Hollywood. Innovative technology, however, could be a formidable differentiation, especially if we were able to reduce the exorbitant cost of animation filmmaking. With this basic analysis in hand, we set up Elixar Studios in 2008. The mission of our venture: To make high quality films based on

Indian mythology and culture, while rewriting the economics of animation filmmaking through technological innovation.

We put together a board of directors early on with people who understood our vision and were able to connect the right dots. Dominique had worked with Steve Jobs and Greg Brandeau (CTO of Pixar) at NeXT. Greg and Dominique became the first two board members of Elixar, and they immediately brought on John Lasseter, one of the founders of Pixar and director of studio hits like *Toy Story*. They then brought on Brad Bird, the two-time Academy Award–winning director of *The Incredibles* and *Ratatouille*. With such a rich and varied group of mentors to guide the project, we were able to gain funding through Disney's venture capital arm, Steamboat Ventures. Disney would distribute all our films, as they did with Pixar.

We started with technology. For two years, our team of top-notch computer scientists worked in Silicon Valley to build new 3-D computer animation software. With multi-core computing making headway, the software was optimized with inherent parallelism to run at previously unknown speeds. The technology was also capable of an unprecedented level of automation. Characters walked, ran, swam, flew, somersaulted, threw javelins, or wielded swords and tridents with software commands and hardware rendering, and without much human intervention. What took 15 hours to do with previous generations of animation technologies could now be done in 15 minutes – offering our creatives more latitude for experimentation, while simultaneously shrinking the time required to make a film.

We patented every angle of the technology and had no intention of selling it as a tool. We were going to use our own technology to make our own movies. But first we would need a creative director à la Lasseter. For this, John nominated one of his protégés from Pixar, Rini Chaudhury, who studied at his alma mater, the California College of Arts (CCA), and had worked under him on *Cars* and *Wall-E*. She was raised in the US, but her family was of

Indian origin, so she knew many of the stories and was fascinated by such mythical characters as the polyandrous princess, Draupadi, and the skull-garland sporting goddess, Kali.

We set up two centers for our animation teams: one in Ahmedabad, close to the National Institute of Design, and the other in Shantiniketan, affiliated with Viswabharati University. A month after the Viswabharati center opened, I went back to check on the progress, and I found one animator after another glued to their screens, their eyes intent, unaware of my presence.

"Are they playing online games?" I asked their manager. "They look so focused, so addicted."

The manager, a transplant from Pixar's Emeryville studio, smiled and gestured to me. "Come, let me show you."

I followed him to a workstation where we watched a young man create the entire battle scene of Durga versus Mahishashura in front of our eyes.

"Impossible," I said aloud.

"Not anymore."

No other animation studio in India, or abroad, had access to our technology, so word spread through the animation community that Elixar was the company to work for. In Internet message boards, animators were chatting about Elixar's miracle, itching to get their hands on it. But the only way to do so – work for us. We started getting resumes from CCA, Rhode Island School of Design, NYU's Tisch, and numerous other prestigious art schools. All the applicants were clamoring to play with our software, even if it meant moving to India.

I tried to suppress my smile, but it was hard not to have fun with the turn of events. American animators wanting to move to a small town in India? This might be fodder enough for a film itself.

In 2008, as we started work on the technology, we had also started working on our first story, *Kali*. We had to assemble a team of storytellers who knew how to write fast-moving yet sensitive scripts with complex characters. I had attended Robert McKee's Story Seminar in which McKee offered an in-depth analysis and framework for storytelling. Almost every successful screenwriter in Hollywood, from Lasseter to Akiva Goldsman (*A Beautiful Mind*), had taken the course. I agreed in principle with McKee's emphasis on story over spectacle, and we structured Elixar according to that philosophy.

We created story teams of experienced Hollywood screenwriters paired with Indian writers who knew the local texture, culture, and heritage. Brad brought in Tom McCarthy, who had worked on the *Up* script, to provide overall guidance from our advisory board. We also recruited Sabrina Dhawan, best known for writing Mira Nair's widely acclaimed *Monsoon Wedding*. Sabrina, at the time, was teaching at NYU's Tisch School, and she helped us recruit many of our screenwriters over the years. While she and I wrote *Kali*, we trained a team of screenwriters who would become our long-term screenwriting team.

Over the last 10 years, this team has written 10 spectacular features. Five of them were based on the *Mahabharat*. Three more on other Indian epics and mythology (*Ramayan, Bhagavat,* and the *Devi-Puranas*). The ninth was based on Abanindranath Thakur's *Raj Kahini*, set in Rajasthan. And the tenth an adaptation of Shirshendu Mukherji's children's ghost story, *Gnoshai Baganer Bhut*, but superimposed onto the Indian cricket scene.

All films were done in English, for international audiences. Our *Mahabharat* scripts turned out to be a nail-biting political-thriller franchise that quickly amassed its own Harry Potter–like following. In *Kali,* we juxtaposed the gods versus demons battles of the *Devi Puranas* with a distinct humanization of the mythical characters.

Our production budget per film was an unbelievable $25 million, while each film, each year since 2011, has grossed an average of $250 million. But not only have they been lucrative, three out of the 10 have won Oscars for best animated feature film, securing for Elixar a brand that these days, automatically draws a global audience.

Pixar finally has a competitor.

Today, we have turned our attention towards Europe, China, Japan, and the US, where we hope to develop films with local talent, weaving local stories. Our Italian studio is already deep into a Julius Caesar script, as well as one on Cleopatra and Mark Anthony. In Paris, we have a team working on the story of Napoleon's first love, Desirée, who went on to become the queen of Sweden. And in Athens, an effort is underway to give life to Homer's *Odyssey*, as well as Helen of Troy, who like Elixar itself, launched a thousand ships.

FRAMED IVORY

Once Elixar cracked open the narrative wealth of India, I began to investigate other kindred opportunities. If animation had translated well, how would realism translate? And within that, the components of culture, of landscape, of architecture, and cuisine.

The West had developed a steadily increasing appetite for Indian stories since the end of the millennium. Arundhati Roy won the Booker Prize in 1997 for *God of Small Things*. Jhumpa Lahiri won the Pulitzer for *Interpreter of Maladies* in 2000. In 2002, *Lagaan* was nominated for the foreign language film Oscar. And in 2009, *Slumdog Millionaire* won eight Academy Awards including Best Picture.

As we researched those two opportunities around animation and realism, a third opportunity became evident: a film company focused on Indian "period" stories set in exotic locations, delivering the classical Indian way of life to Western audiences.

My model for Framed Ivory Films drew from a combination of prior experiments. Merchant Ivory Productions, founded in 1961, had often focused on Victorian and Edwardian Britain, adapting the stories of Henry James, E. M. Forster, and others. Flowing from the masterful writing hand of Ruth Prawer Jhabvala, James Ivory and Ismail Merchant brought to the screen such powerful stories as *A Room with a View, Howard's End,* and *Remains of the Day.*

Bollywood had also indulged in period pieces. From Indian classics, Pradeep Sarkar and Sanjay Leela Bansali made *Parineeta* and *Devdas,* respectively. Rituparno Ghosh made a rather poor rendition of *Chokher Bali*, in Bengali. Deepa Mehta made the splendid *Water.* Ashutosh Gowarikar made the lovely *Jodha Akbar*, set in Rajasthan. Mira Nair made an atrocious, though beautifully shot, *Kama Sutra.* However, none of these films, except *Kama Sutra*, were in English, and my observation was that with growing global interest in India, an audience was fast developing. The "poor India" was already well known through the *City of Joy*–type stories. Now came the time for the India of palaces, *havelis*, exotic costumes, and grand style – an India that Bollywood had long portrayed.

Framed Ivory's India would be clothed in such style, culture, architecture, and color, but without the seven songs and three- to four-hour run time. Framed Ivory's stories would be honed to a sharp, Hollywood edge. But with one magnificent alteration: each of our films would fall within a $5 million budget, but attempt to gross a minimum of $50 million – a 1000% return on investment.

At the back of my mind was Mira Nair's delightful comedy, *Monsoon Wedding*, which was made on a $160,000 production budget, but went on to gross over $30 million at the box office. The key: *Monsoon Wedding* was in English, which opened up Indian film to a whole new audience that other powerful films, such as *Water,* made in Hindi, were unable to access.

To further ensure Western patronage, we used several other tricks as well – the most important being dubbing. Many Indian actors and actresses spoke English with a heavy accent, bogging down international access. So, inspired by Rituporno Ghosh's dubbing of Aisharya Rai and Raima Sen in *Chokher Bali*, we dubbed our Indian actors' voices such that clean, polished, accent-free English flowed from their mouths.

For the stories they told, we went first to the territory I knew best: Bengali classics. Tagore, Saratchandra, Bankimchandra, Tarashankar, Sharadindu, Bimal Mitra. Even modern writers like Bani Basu, Sunil Ganguly, and Budhhadeb Guha had written period stories worth filming. Ganguly's *Prothom Alo*, for example, brought to life renaissance Bengal with all its ambience, a perfect backdrop for the story of Tagore's love for his sister-in-law, Kadambari. We also got original screenplays written against the backdrops of Rajasthan, Agra. Then a poignant love story in Lucknow. A murder mystery set in Ujjain. A thriller in Hyderabad. And a disillusionment plot in the Himalayas. Finally, Indian actors would play on the world stage, telling stories of their own.

In 2010, we produced our first film based on Bankimchandra Chattarjee's *Debi Chaudhurani*, my all-time favorite, featuring a profoundly enigmatic bandit queen, originally captured but later nurtured by the erudite leader of a gang that looted the British along the waterways of Bengal. The two-hour English-language film was directed by Sandeep Ray, who realized his legendary father, Satyajit Ray's, dream of making a film based on the story. It won the Palme d'Or at Cannes and grossed $163 million.

In 2011, we did two films. First, Sharadindu Bandopadhyay's *Zinder Bandi* (Prisoner of Zind), and the second, Bankimchandra's *Kapalkundala*. Each grossed a neat $55 million. In 2012, we did Bimal Mitra's *Shaheb Bibi o Golam*, Saratchandra's *Srikanta*, Bankimchandra's *Rajsingha* (set in Rajasthan), Dinabandhu Mitra's *Nil Darpan* (set against the backdrop of the Indigo revolution), and Narayan Sanyal's *Sutanuka* (set in Khajuraho). The five films grossed a total of over $450 million.

By 2015, Framed Ivory Films had become an international sensation. Our following snaked out theater doors from London to San Francisco. To audiences tired of consuming the same ol' Hollywood fodder, we brought fresh, intricate stories from our heritage with rich layering that only an ancient culture like India could offer. So that today, a previously unknown India has been revealed to the world. Audiences have gathered en masse, filling the house, oohing and aahing between fists of popcorn, in support of this new billion-dollar film genre.

KANISHKA RAJA

I had, for a long time, believed that one of the twenty-first century's best ventures was the Harry Potter franchise. Apple and Google have also been colossal franchises, but the fantasy world of Harry Potter has woven magic. As if pulled from a hat, J. K. Rowling's marvelous boy-hero launched a whole generation of youngsters down paths of reading, courage, friendship, and adventure, while for Rowling herself a path of great riches. Let's take a look at the numbers:

On July 14, 2005, the BBC reported, "The global popularity of the books, films and games is estimated to have made the Harry Potter brand worth $1 billion. More than 265 million copies of the books have been sold in 200 countries. Author J. K. Rowling, whose rise to fame itself is a marketing executive's dream, is reputedly now Britain's wealthiest woman [not Queen Elizabeth]. Waterstone's booksellers estimates that on the first day of its release, the *Half-Blood Prince* will sell at least two million copies in the UK and more than 10 million worldwide. Meanwhile, supermarket giant Tesco estimates that it will sell 300 copies a minute when the book finally goes on sale in the early hours of Saturday morning."

Four days later, on July 18, 2005, the BBC reported, "The new Harry Potter book has beaten sales records on both sides of the

Atlantic, selling almost nine million copies in its first 24 hours. *Harry Potter and the Half-Blood Prince* sold 6.9 million copies in the US and more than two million copies in the UK, beating all previous Potter records. Estimates from Nielsen BookScan revealed that 2,009,574 copies of *Harry Potter and the Half-Blood Prince* had been sold within 24 hours of release. US sales of the sixth Harry Potter book have generated more than $100 million (£57 million) in revenue across the weekend – more than the combined box office sales of hit films, *Charlie and the Chocolate Factory* and *The Wedding Crashers*."

By June 2008, the book series, by then translated into 67 languages, had sold more than 400 million copies, with the last four books crushing previous records as the fastest-selling books in history. With blockbuster films and tie-in merchandise galore, the Harry Potter brand had risen to close to $10 billion.

Yes, hundreds of millions of people in the UK and US appreciated the boy hero, but what about the many hundreds of millions in India? No doubt, scores of Indian kids loved Harry Potter, but I felt they also deserved their own hero. He came to me, gradually, through dreams, through McKee-style story design, and often, by digging through history and mythology. Eventually, I christened him Kanishka Raja after the second-century emperor – a powerful Kushan king and conqueror and, eventually, a proponent of Buddhism.

Kanishka Raja became the hero of my own series of fantasy thrillers based in second-century Purushapur. Kanishka Raja, of course, had extraordinary powers. He could travel back in time to explore the mysteries of his predecessors – Alexander the Great, Chandragupta Maurya, Emperor Ashoka, and Chandragupta's crafty minister, Chanakya. Furthermore, he could dialogue and discourse with them, learning from their experience, reliving their battles and political maneuverings, while charting the course of his own destiny, the destiny of his empire.

Once I zeroed in on Kanishka as my hero, I decided to turn the book and the film businesses on their heels in building the franchise. Instead of taking an advance for my franchise, I raised venture capital with the intent of doing a book, a film, and a game in quick succession. Whereas the public had to wait four years from the 1997 release of J. K. Rowling's first Harry Potter book to the first movie adaptation in 2001, the first Kanishka Raja book, *Time Capsule*, released in January 2010, the online multiplayer game based on the book released in June 2010, and the film released in November of that same year.

The book was published and distributed worldwide by Hachette, with whom I had previously done my *Entrepreneur Journeys* series in India. However, after studying the financial structure of the book business for several years, I negotiated a more favorable royalty structure of 40% for the 10-book series. Normally, publishers offered royalties in the 7%–15% range, which I simply refused to accept. Hachette saw the potential of the franchise since the films and games would give the books great market pull – so there was little argument. Besides, they had become accustomed to my disruptive ideas by this time.

The classic channels were quick to fall into place. Films were distributed by Disney, whom I'd worked with on Elixar, and who became a major shareholder in the franchise. Hachette also took an equity stake in the deal, having understood that we were about to spectacularly restructure their traditional (and archaic) business! Then I invited my friend Gus Tai at Trinity Ventures to hop on to the Kanishka Raja *Time Capsule*.

Over lunch at the Sundeck, I said to him ominously, "It's time, Gus."

"Time for what?" he laughed.

"To bring to bear those years of thinking on the book business, the film business, edutainment, gaming, story. Remember McKee?"

"Ah, yes. And Harry Potter. You've been talking about it for years! Have you started writing the book?"

I had not only started writing the first book of the series, I had actually finished several drafts with various endings. The truth was, I could not come to terms with any of the endings. I applied all that I learned from McKee, but every time I made a decision, I would have a nightmare that books were not selling, that Hachette was canceling their contract, that my 10-year-old Kanishka Raja was looking at me with accusing eyes.

But this period of raw dread passed in time.

Time Capsule launched to a sensational reception. The game launched six months later. BBC was the first to do a major story on the phenomenon. In a segment showing children being called to dinner repeatedly before their parents finally had to come and shut off the computer, they narrated how Indian prince Kanishka Raja had captured the imagination of children all over the world. How kids were playing as Alexander, strategizing world domination, or as the Buddha, promoting nonviolence through social media. And surprise of all surprises, they were reading, scouring the books for clues on how to win the games.

Time Capsule had sold two million copies worldwide, accruing some $8 million in revenues in 2011. The film, which cost us $15 million to produce, brought in $45 million at the box office that year. Six months later we released the game, and within three months it garnered some 200,000 players, bringing in an additional $2 million in revenues. Without tallying merchandise or licensing deals, we already posted $55 million in revenue.

We released a book, a movie, and a game every other year from then on. By 2015, the three Kanishka Raja books had cumulatively sold 220 million copies; the third film garnered $346 million in the box office; and the games were at the fingertips of 20 million players. Today in 2020, five books, five films, and five games later, the Kanishka Raja franchise is now valued at $5 billion.

So what is the magic of Kanishka Raja? This, my friends, is something I don't have to tell you. You've read the books, seen the films, and played the games yourselves.

BIOSCOPE

In December 2005, Dominique and I traveled through North Bengal. We touched great mountains, deep valleys, shimmering rivers. We saw great forests waking with dawn and returning to slumber at nightfall. We touched the brink of life in the jungle. Not much was different here than in primordial times. A forest guard lived in a small shack at the mouth of a leopard- and elephant-infested forest. If he died, another took his place. Man survived here against the ever-present wild, where elephants rampaged through the forests, destroying crops, even killing villagers as they tried in vain to keep them at bay with mere firecrackers.

It was a place unparalleled for both its raw beauty and brutality. The scenery of tea gardens, betel nut woods, bay leaf plants, and cardamom bushes slowly rolled into hills, then mountains as we climbed towards Lava, at 7,000 feet, a splendid little Himalayan village far out by the Bhutan border. Surrounded by layers of Himalayan panorama, sitting in a small cottage facing the hue of the setting sun, we could not help but ponder the life of the villagers. At sundown, the village quiets, then sleeps. There was nothing to do. No cinema. No theater. No club. Low voltage electricity inadequate even for television. Consequently, alcohol was often a friendly companion to pass time around a fire.

Without enough light to read in our cottage, Dominique and I started discussing first the pure numbers – there were approximately 600,000 villages in India, with 600 million people living in such limited opportunity settings – and next the opportunity: an alternative entertainment vehicle, one more appealing than alcohol. Thus began our journey of building a chain of "community screens" throughout the heartland of India. Thus began Bioscope.

At the heart of Bioscope was a media server containing some 5,000 Bollywood movies with appropriate licensing rights, a projector, and a screen. Rather than full-fledged movie theaters, ours are akin to an elaborate home theater setup. We rent large rooms within each village to seat 35–40 people – effectively small movie theaters.

In five years, we built a presence in 100,000 villages. Come sundown, village women would don their best saris and drag their husbands to the Bioscope. Initially, the husbands complained. But soon, they were more excited than their women at the prospect of a swaying Ash or a swinging Hrithik.

Although we made arrangements with several banks to finance these franchises with microloans, our business plan was not to build a nonprofit. We wanted to build a media channel to reach the few hundred million people of rural India without television sets, and therefore off the regular media grid. Gradually, we hooked our franchisees up with a central server, such that we could transmit advertisements and other video clips before films and during intermissions. These advertising slots we sold to our network of corporations at a premium. And as our penetration numbers climbed, as we leapt from Maharashtra screens to Manipur screens, the advertising rates we commanded also skyrocketed.

Meanwhile, an interesting social dynamic developed in the villages around Bioscope. Villagers started treating the screenings as their primary place to see and be seen. People started showing up an hour or two before the show to mingle, chat, and match-make. After the movie, people hung around to discuss how the villain,

Chhote Malik, seduced the unsuspecting Karina at the cinema. "*Saale...*," they hissed. They hummed one of the seven songs from the film. Some danced. Soon, there was a party each night after the screening. Then cafés sprung up, where rumor mills spun and Coke found new customers; where marriages got brokered and Pepsi introduced new brands; where hearts got broken and Frito Lay got munched.

As the community bonded, Bioscope's power to influence word of mouth increased exponentially. Not only were our advertisers aware of this power, the politicians were too. We became one of the primary channels of political advertising, as well as an excellent channel for spreading educational messages on topics as disparate as birth control, reproductive health, women's empowerment, microfinance, and micro-franchise.

Banks were advertising heavily with Bioscope, spreading the message of mobile banking, as well as offering microfinance loans. In fact, we started collaborating with other micro-franchise ventures like Gagori, Palanquin, Camellia, and Patami. We made it infinitely easier for them to recruit new franchisees and scale their businesses.

Of course, we had programs that tied into these ancillary ventures. For example, we started our own "citizen journalism" effort, where each village had a reporter trained to capture video success stories about micro-entrepreneurs. Men and women like designer Chameli Rai and pharmacist Guru Desai. Success stories from one village were then played not only in that village, but in neighboring and distant villages alike, making celebrities of our micro-heroes. In the last decade, we have helped groom almost three million new micro-entrepreneurs in fields spanning furniture to candles to solar energy, and we have helped shape the sociopolitical consciousness of rural India. Not bad for so-called micro!

We also created independent programming about the sociopolitical issues that citizens of a successful democracy should understand, such as freedom of speech and rights of expression. Our philosophy of development through entrepreneurship was widely propagated, and leaders with policies supporting entrepreneurship development were offered opportunities to communicate with our audience through video conferencing.

In 2020, having penetrated 300,000 villages, we stepped back to take stock. Bioscope looks a lot like the early days of the movie theater – dust particles swimming in projector light – but fused with modern concepts like the video library, digital storage, media server, portable projectors, user-generated content, and citizen-journalism.

And this fusion has fundamentally altered the cultural fabric of rural India, infusing it with a sense of engagement and empowerment, while Bioscope has blossomed to become one of modern India's most cherished media channels.

NCTV

In the twenty-first century, India was embracing consumerism at a frantic pace. To continue at this pace, these consumer brands desperately needed to reach more remote consumers, with whom it was harder to achieve deep brand engagement than with urban consumers.

Cricket was one of the primary unifying factors for the country. At the same time, I found it frustrating that when there were sports on the tube, 95% of the time it was cricket. However, on the streets and in the fields, young people kicked soccer balls, arched basketballs towards the rim, and sent badminton corks flying as well. There was a clear a gap between what was on TV and the diverse array the youth were playing. NCTV is a media company we built around the core concept of non-cricket television, funded by ESPN.

As in prior years, India put up a pathetic show in the 2008 Beijing Olympics. Athletes were sent to compete in archery, badminton, boxing, hockey, judo, rowing, sailing, shooting, swimming, table tennis, tennis, track and field, and men's freestyle wrestling. In soccer, basketball, and the bulk of other Olympic sports, India failed to qualify. For all of these entrants, India won a total of three medals, a gold in men's 10-meter air rifle shooting and a bronze each in men's middleweight boxing and 66-kilogram men's freestyle wrestling. In contrast, China won 100 medals, and the United States 110.

Having studied how Jagmohan Dalmiya transformed Indian cricket from a negative-five-lakhs-a-year sport to a mega-money spinner, I was curious about how to build the same following for other sports, evolving them into similarly big-money media events. Our analysis was that an exclusive non-cricket television channel, coupled with a systematic effort in coaching, training, and audience-building, would be an apt first step.

We targeted 10 disciplines: aquatics, athletics, badminton, boxing, gymnastics, hockey, table tennis, tennis, shooting, and wrestling. Each discipline had 50 training academies spread deep into small towns in hopes of accessing the untapped talent of India. This decentralization gave us the opportunity to engage audiences in less accessible parts of the country, including those who could not attend major sporting events at the Eden Gardens in Kolkata or the Wankhede Stadium in Mumbai. So instead of building audiences by pure televised inclusion, we built viewers by making them participants, players, addicts.

Each academy was a residential training and competition venue, complete with modern amenities for our 100 athletes in training. A world-class foreign coach, aided by 10 Indian coaches, spearheaded each program. Kids, ages 10 and up, were culled from each academy's surrounding region.

To build our television audience, we looked to the reality TV phenomenon that was, in 2009, sweeping the world. Reality television saw an explosion in the early 2000s. *Survivor*, *American Idol*, and *Dancing With the Stars* were all top-rated series on American television. In sports, reality programs typically created a sporting competition among athletes attempting to establish themselves in that sport. *The Club*, in 2002, was one of the first shows to fuse sports with reality TV, with the audience helping to select which players played each week by voting for their favorites. *The Big*

Break was a popular golf reality show. *The Contender* was a boxing show in which, sadly, a contestant committed suicide after being eliminated.

In our version, every academy offered a built-in cast of 100 or more characters, their families, personal stories, failures, and triumphs. Think, in its earliest form, of the award-winning documentary *Hoop Dreams*, and then fast-forward to ABC's hit, *Dancing With the Stars*. Our framework of 500 small-town academies crossing 10 disciplines became a major phenomenon in each region's entertainment calendar – ripe with local teams to cheer on, local heroes to worship, local stars to build, and local gossip to pass from ear to ear.

The shows were rolled out in 2010 on a region-by-region basis, in local languages, and 20 academies bloomed across eastern and western India in just one discipline: tennis. At bus stands, in schools, and on rickshaws, suddenly kids with tennis rackets became a common sighting.

Signs of Coca-Cola, Pepsi, Disney, and Airtel were hoisted onto the academy rooftops, presiding over neighborhoods as proud sponsors of local centers. The centers themselves stood as modern stately buildings, often situated amidst fields of maize or rice paddies. In amenities, they were state of the art, fitted with myriad forms of equipment for stretching, toning, and aerobics, alongside ball-machines, racket-stringing facilities, and video analysis rooms.

Each academy sponsor contributed Rs. 1 crore ($200,000) for a branded center for three years, and Rs. 50 lakhs ($100,000) a year in ongoing sponsorship. These were branded as Coca-Cola Tennis Academies, Airtel Tennis Academies, and so on. Annual sponsorship included extensive physical branding on location, as well as on the athletes' outfits. Television advertising rights were sold separately.

Our rollout ramped quickly after the first 20 academies. By 2012, we had 50 tennis centers, and 20 centers each for badminton, table tennis, and hockey. In each sport, some athletes from our academies were competing and winning at the state and national championships, which we televised for those back home to enjoy.

In fact, when 14-year-old Rukmini Gupta won the table tennis women's singles title at the Hyderabad Nationals in 2014, her entire hometown of Burhanpur in Madhya Pradesh came to the train station with marigold garlands to welcome her back.

By 2015, all 10 disciplines were up and running, and by 2018, every discipline had 50 academies. In tennis, the entire Indian Davis Cup team was made up of NCTV athletes, one of whom had advanced to the Wimbledon semifinal. Players in all 10 disciplines were sweeping state and national titles. In the 2018 Asian Games, India won 191 medals, a remarkable improvement over the 51 they earned in 2006.

Today we look toward the 2020 Olympics, to be held in New Delhi, confident that India will medal in at least five disciplines. Meanwhile, NCTV, with 25 million viewers, has become India's most exciting, inspiring sports channel, masterminding and chronicling the story of the country's rise as a credible sporting nation.

TORQUATO TASSO

As India blossomed into a global player, I felt it needed to do more than develop greater markets for its own products and services; it needed to open its domestic purchasing power to other countries' products and services. A thriving economy well connected through international trade, exchange, and goodwill was my vision, rather than the protected, highly regulated, isolated land it had so long been. We knew from the Nehru era, from over 50 years of failed policies, that protectionism was not the answer.

One product that India had very little understanding of was wine. Instead, Indians were accustomed to drinking whiskey and rum, while wine remained an unfamiliar and expensive outsider. In 2006, Indian winemakers sold roughly 940,000 cases of wine domestically and 60,000 cases overseas, up from 530,000 and 30,000 respectively in 2003, according to industry figures. Major cities like Mumbai, Delhi, Chennai, Kolkata, Pune, Bangalore, and Hyderabad accounted for 80% of this demand. By comparison, American vintners shipped 217 million cases to domestic markets in 2007, and another 50 million cases overseas.

I thought it would be an interesting venture to market the concept of wine, and through that, develop diplomatic relationships with several major wine-producing countries including the United States (California and Oregon), France, Italy, Spain, Argentina, Chile, South Africa, Australia, and New Zealand. With that thought, in 2010, we launched an exclusive club in Mumbai called Torquato Tasso. A club positioned as Mumbai's wine lover's destination, stocked with the best cellar in all of India, drawing from vineyards the world over.

My own relationship with wine had developed over 20 years, though during trips to Buenos Aires, I developed a special interest in Argentine wine. I remember fondly a small Recoleta store on Avenida Alvear called Grand Cru, whose staff pointed out to me many a gem, including the Doña Paula Malbec from Mendoza.

However, my real interest in Argentina – which drew me south on many occasions – was the country's ever-enigmatic art form: the Argentine tango. So, along with our regular tastings, roundtables, and apprenticeships, we decided to offer tango as entertainment at Torquato Tasso. In fact, we named the club after a famous live music venue in Buenos Aires that I knew and loved.

Tango masters were culled from the barrios of Buenos Aires and cities around the world to teach our members their dance. The first we brought to India was Florencia Taccetti, who spoke fluent English, but was also classically trained under maestros like Miguel Angel Zotto, Miguel Balmaceda, Graciela Gonzalez, Juan Bruno, Antonio Todaro, Gustavo Naveira, and Mingo Pugliese. I had met her on my first visit in 1998. And 12 years later, Florencia arrived in Mumbai with one of her talented students, Marcos, to partner her for lessons and shows.

Their first show at the club started with Florencia and Marcos performing to a set of dramatic arrangements from Osvaldo Pugliese's excellent repertoire. The audience at Torquato Tasso, their fingers laced around goblets of Mendoza, Bordeaux, and Montalcino wines, was spellbound. Most of them had never seen Argentine tango danced with such precision and elegance.

Our groundbreaking Mumbai Torquato Tasso drew 4,000 members in 2010. The membership fee was Rs. 5,000 ($100) per person. To these 4,000 members and their guests, we sold close to 200,000 bottles (over 16,000 cases) that year, while to our surprise, the dance lessons generated another Rs. 8 crores ($1.6 million).

Torquato Tasso had captured the imagination of Mumbai's elite in a way that nothing else had in recent memory. It became the place to be and be seen. Entertainment columnists went wild. *Femina* created a special column called "Tasso Watch" in which they endlessly reported on which tycoon, cricket star, or Bollywood actress was at Torquato Tasso on which night, and what wine they drank. *Times of India* did a feature story on the best tango dancers seen on the Torquato Tasso floor, asking, "Was it Hrithik Roshan or Saif Ali Khan?" And *Sommelier India* had a special report on the wines at Torquato Tasso in every issue.

With the wind at our back, we opened a second club in New Delhi in 2011. On opening night, Gustavo Naveira and Giselle Anne, two of tango's most beloved maestros, performed. The crowd was mesmerized. Gustavo's experiments with *nuevo tango* had introduced a sense of dynamism into the tango world, and in Delhi, he and Giselle Anne moved across the floor with electric intensity.

The following year we opened in Bangalore and Kolkata. Chennai, Hyderabad, Pune, and a second club in Mumbai opened in 2013. The decision to open the second club in Mumbai was based on the fact that our dance floors were getting too crowded – people could not show off their *ochos*, *ganchos*, and *sentadas* – newly acquired tango steps that looked oh so sexy!

The year 2014 was our year of expansion. We opened second clubs in Delhi, Kolkata, Chennai, Pune, Bangalore, and new clubs in Jamshedpur, Ahmedabad, and Nagpur. At 16 clubs in 10 cities, we were truly a phenomenon. The Indian elite soaked up wine from Bordeaux, Burgundy, Marlborough, Rioja, and Stellenbosch, and they danced tango in its myriad forms – milonguero, salon, milonga traspie, vals, candombe.

Today, in 2020, the phenomenon has crawled over India like a virus, spreading first through its Torquato Tasso host and finally into the mainstream. Indians not only drink wine and dance at Torquato Tasso, they do it in clubs and at home, growing India into one of the largest wine importers in the world.

The numbers – our numbers – are staggering.

Torquato Tasso boasts some 128 clubs and over half a million members. Membership alone generates 10% of our revenues. We sell over two million cases, or 25 million bottles, of wine, generating another 50% of our revenue. Then the restaurant and dance lessons generate the remaining 40%. Torquato Tasso, India's very own entertainment franchise, is a billion-dollar enterprise – a brand that over a million people enjoy, another five million aspire to join, and some 50 million read about in lifestyle magazines who chronicle our swirling tango floors that you have seen for yourselves!

EPILOGUE

India, maybe more so than any other country, has a critical decade ahead. Infrastructure remains in a precarious state. Relentless urbanization has taken a decimating aesthetic and environmental toll, rendering cities near unlivable. The education system is failing to educate. The 6%–8% GDP growth can only be sustained if infrastructure develops at a similar pace, and if the ongoing environmental disaster can be reined in and then reversed.

While I said at the outset that entrepreneurs alone can carry the development mission forward, there is no doubt that the government must also demonstrate political will to bring about systemic change. Entrepreneurs will need help. Help through policies that dictate the construction of solar and hydro smart grids, as well as canals to engage in water diplomacy. And help from governments in bringing about aggressive privatization of ports and airports.

Vision India 2020 is, therefore, just as much for those in government who are serious about moving India forward as it is for entrepreneurs on the brink. And just as much as it is for Indian policymakers and Indian entrepreneurs, it must also be for those neighboring India, both friend and foe: Pakistan, Bangladesh, Sri Lanka, Nepal, Bhutan. I am convinced that for India's development to proceed undeterred, the rest of the South Asian countries must join in the advance. For each have critical dependencies with India, and India with them.

Jute, for instance, is as much a strength of India as it is of Bangladesh. Where, after all, do the plains of Bengal end and those of Bangladesh begin? An entrepreneur taking on a jute project has no reason not to include the crop from Bangladesh. And any water desalination project along the coast of Gujarat must take into account Pakistan's needs, just as it considers Rajasthan's. Too long has the region been divided in political and ideological quarrel when these common gains could advance the region's holistic health.

By 2050, India will have a population of 1.6 billion people, the largest in the world. While this is an enormous problem, from the point of view of entrepreneurs and marketers elsewhere in the world, India's immense consumer population is also a phenomenally attractive business opportunity. But only if India allows the international business community free access to its markets, enticing entrepreneurs and investors from around the world to bring their products into India. Increased diplomatic relations depend upon such trade. If French wine, for example, became popular in India, it would create many jobs back home in France. Perhaps Africa, Latin America, and Indonesia will develop on the wings of supplying minerals to India. And perhaps on the wings of such trade so too will grow the working relationships between India and the greater globe.

At the same time, India needs to import more than goods. Expertise in its areas of weakness also need to be brought in – one of them being marketing, and a second, design. These are disciplines that the Americans, the Japanese, the French, and the Italians excel in. India must welcome, and learn from, the immense talents of these countries.

In 2020, I envision a more international India. An open India. An India engaged with the world – not imperialistic, but diplomatic and benevolent. An India capable of complementing its natural strengths with those of its international collaborators.

A high-velocity India unencumbered by mindless bureaucracy. A thinking India that can envision its own products, rather than blindly executing on American specs. And finally, a bold, confident India, having shaken off centuries of servility to stand on its own two feet and look out upon its own infinite possibilities.

Is that India so far away? Ten years, at most.

Other books by Sramana Mitra
Now available from Amazon.com

Entrepreneur Journeys, Volume One

Entrepreneur Journeys begins with a simple idea: technology start-up success, and the knowledge required to achieve it, is out there to be leveraged by anyone who is willing to listen. Using her own intimate knowledge of the entrepreneurial world, in this book renowned strategist and *Forbes* columnist Sramana Mitra captures the stories of entrepreneurs that have come before to help those who are looking to learn. Offering readers an inside view of how to navigate an entrepreneurial path, Mitra synthesizes candid conversations with her own incisive analysis, to create a unique set of case studies.

Truly a book that distinguishes itself from the crowded business-book marketplace, Mitra has written a text that is accessible through its story-telling narrative, and at the same time academic in its depth of insight.

Some praise:

"Inspiration awaits readers in this volume of interviews with entrepreneurs. *Entrepreneur Journeys* will provide great insight into the questions and answers behind a start-up business. It succeeds in sharing the enthusiasm and sense of adventure of these technological pioneers."
  -Kirkus Discoveries

"Entrepreneurship is not a career. It is a way of life. And what better way to learn about it than to listen to people who have done it, successfully, and to learn about their lives in that fast lane? In a carefully structured set of interviews, Sramana Mitra gives the readers an opportunity to discover their paths, their successes, their setbacks sometimes, and the joys of meeting the immense challenges that have been theirs in a dizzying world where technical competence and management skills have allowed them to leave a deep and lasting mark."
  -Professor Elisabeth Paté-Cornell
Chair, Department of Management Science and Engineering, Stanford University

More praise for *Entrepreneur Journeys*:

"Enjoyed *Entrepreneur Journeys* and found it worthwhile. The stories are inspiring and could have a significant influence on a student of entrepreneurship or an aspiring entrepreneur. To paraphrase a trite phrase; 'Yes, you can!' The stories are more than inspiration though. The insightful questions and the thoughtful answers give much guidance, and general wisdom. The book occupies a nearly empty niche between lightweight collections of anecdotes and ponderous but often irrelevant academic research. A great opportunity to come close to sitting with masters and learning directly."

-Barrett Hazeltine, Professor of Engineering Emeritus, Brown University

"Sramana Mitra is herself a symbol of everything that is great about America: a geek, an entrepreneur, an immigrant, a leader. In *Entrepreneur Journeys* she has taken on the task of modeling how entrepreneurs transform economies into resilient, growing systems that provide a future for our children."

-Stewart Alsop, General Partner, Alsop Louie Partners

"Sramana Mitra has gifted us with the first hand stories of industry legends who have succeeded with a combination of fierce resolve, self-reliance, and a willingness to buck conventional wisdom. The next generation of entrepreneurs has an invaluable reference guide on how their predecessors have succeeded."

-Rick Rommel, Senior Vice President Emerging Business, Best Buy

Entrepreneur Journeys, Volume Two:
Bootstrapping: Weapon of Mass Reconstruction

In a world battered by economic crisis, Sramana Mitra believes entrepreneurship is the only sustainable path forward to a healthy economic world order. And core to the success of entrepreneurial ventures today is the invigorating art of bootstrapping. She takes aim at this essential route along the roadmap to startup success in the second volume of *Entrepreneur Journeys*. Along with her incisive analysis and commentary, she showcases a dozen successful entrepreneurs and their lessons from the bootstrapping trenches. Overflowing with lively entrepreneurial tangents, theories, and behind-closed-doors-experience, the book rises to the level of economic policy discussion while simultaneously offering practical advice from experienced bootstrappers. Important issues like doing more with less, getting started with little or no capital, and validating the market on the cheap are discussed with the likes of Om Malik of GigaOm and Greg Gianforte of RightNow.

Some praise:

"Sramana Mitra's *Bootstrapping: Weapon of Mass Reconstruction* is a book for our time because it's something real out of Silicon Valley. No more stories about legendary VC fundings of startup-to-IPO in six months. In this, the second volume of *Entrepreneur Journeys*, her focus is on doing more with less, in tune with the times. This book has some fascinating histories of the different paths people take to entrepreneurship, and the difficulties they face. I would only have wished each of the interviews to be longer and deeper, because every story is worth telling."

-Fast Company

"Mitra clearly has a passion for small businesses. This useful volume is largely comprised of interviews with the founders of such companies. Her skilled questioning prompts a discussion of the many issues involved in starting and growing a business. The entrepreneurs share wisdom and insight useful to any budding or existing business owner. The reader will be struck by the vision, inventiveness and sheer determination of these entrepreneurial heroes, who operate businesses that are successful but far below the radar. A highly relevant and timely work on entrepreneurship's role in economic reconstruction."

-Kirkus Discoveries

More praise for *Bootstrapping: Weapon of Mass Reconstruction*:

"I recommend *Bootstrapping: Weapon of Mass Reconstruction* to my MBA students and to anybody planning on, or even just thinking about, starting a business. And also to policymakers. Maybe especially to policymakers. The importance of entrepreneurs to our economy cannot be overemphasized."

-Craig Newmark, Newmark's Door blog
Associate Professor of Economics, North Carolina State University

"Sramana's work on bootstrapped entrepreneurs is an inspiration in these tough economic times. The solutions to our economic problems ultimately lie with the entrepreneur who brings imagination, resourcefulness and good old-fashioned elbow grease to tackle old problems in new ways, create new solutions and new industries. It is all too easy to forget this, particularly when we feed on the depressing daily diet of endless bailouts and hear trillions of dollars being thrown around. A great entrepreneur can do a lot with ten thousand dollars. This book is a good antidote to the depressing mood of these times."

-Sridhar Vembu, CEO of AdventNet and Zoho,
Bootstrapped to over $50 million in annual revenue

"In the end, a true entrepreneur will not be denied. What Sramana captures with simple grace are the riveting personal stories of modern day business alchemists, who mix vision, pragmatism and relentless effort to forge creative new and successful ventures. Her collection of interviews will make for an engaging, educational read, for those in the entrepreneurial space, those considering joining the game and those just plain curious about the formative innovators whose efforts provide outsize social returns of the most concrete and enduring nature."

-Don Hutchison, Silicon Valley Angel Investor

Entrepreneur Journeys, Volume Three
Positioning: How To Test, Validate, And Bring Your Ideas To Market

In *Positioning: How To Test, Validate, And Bring Your Idea To Market*, the third book in her *Entrepreneur Journeys* series, Sramana Mitra offers a close look at the process of sculpting your idea into a sharply defined "go to market" strategy. Clarity, Mitra confirms, is the ultimate tool in building a successful business. But such clarity cannot be purchased or assumed – it requires asking the right questions. Mitra showcases case study after case study of successful entrepreneurs who have answered these questions, analyzed their markets, and defined their value propositions through differentiation, competitive analysis, market sizing, and, among other core elements of a compelling strategic marketing plan, segmentation. The process she takes her readers through is akin to the grilling venture capitalists typically put entrepreneurs through. A grueling test to any business idea, Mitra's book stimulates a due diligence exercise, which no matter if you are bootstrapping or raising venture capital, you must put yourself through to avoid wasting precious years and scarce resources.

Some praise:

"At the beginning of 2009, I found myself without a VP of Marketing in a young start-up company and a new product coming out of the door that would radically change the positioning of the company. I had been introduced to Sramana by a VC who said, 'you have to meet this great lady just to know her.' I contacted her to help me redo the positioning of the company. She did an excellent job in a short period of time using her crisp methodology that has now positioned the company for success. There is no better person to write a book on positioning. In this new series, she lays out the requirements for positioning and uses real world people and companies to illustrate her points. She is a no nonsense leader in our industry that must be listened to."

-*Mark B. Hoffman*
Chairman and CEO, Enquisite; Founder CEO, Sybase; CEO, CommerceOne

More praise for *Positioning: How To Test, Validate, And Bring Your Ideas To Market*:

"Too many entrepreneurs allow their passion to drive them to take action rather than to distill their wisdom. This leads many to jump right into building out generic business functions and pursuing generic strategies. What I've seen over the years is that the most successful entrepreneurs are the ones that pause to deeply understand what market potential they exactly want to unleash. They then set out and test and evolve. Sramana, in her book *Positioning: How To Test, Validate, And Bring Your Ideas To Market*, provides the critical case studies that highlight how entrepreneurs should continually self-evaluate and refine their ideas. It's a great reference."

-*Gus Tai*
General Partner, Trinity Ventures

"Many start-up companies dissipate precious energy and capital without ever reaching a point of clear market traction. Too often, their failure stems from their inability to operationalize their vision into a compelling value proposition targeted at clearly defined customer segments. Sramana Mitra's book *Positioning: How To Test, Validate, And Bring Your Idea To Market* combines personalized vignettes of passionate entrepreneurs who, through trial, errors and sheer determination, have managed to integrate this important lesson across the defining dimensions of the emerging Web 3.0 environment. Aspiring entrepreneurs and experienced venture capitalists alike will benefit from this compilation of focused interviews and will want to test their own enterprises against the scrutiny of Sramana's probing questions."

-*Eric Benhamou*
Chairman 3Com; former CEO, 3Com & Palm; CEO, Benhamou Global Ventures

"Sramana Mitra combines the analytical and questioning skills of a Silicon Valley venture capitalist with cases studies of how successful entrepreneurs used that intense examination to find clarity. The author takes a holistic approach to marketing that examines the path of the product from the idea stage to its final market positioning. Sramana Mitra points out that an idea must be differentiated, and must be able to be targeted with laser accuracy at a specific market segment. Knowing the potential market prior to launch will save both time and money for an entrepreneur. Through the very intensive questioning technique, provided in the book, any idea can be given the same fundamental analysis expected by venture capitalists and other investors. The result is a clarity of vision that will lead to success."

-*Wayne Hurlbert, Blog Business World blog*

"Another feature that I have found to be especially valuable in this series, is the no-nonsense approach to management that these entrepreneurs, forced to sail so harrowingly close to the wind, are compelled to learn and to apply so effectively in their rapidly growing companies."

-*Jim Stroup, Managing Leadership blog*

"Before you get too far down the line with your 'next big idea', a reading of *Positioning* might do wonders to help you narrow your focus and improve your chances of success."

-*Thomas Duff, Duffbert's Random Musings blog*

"I enjoyed *Positioning* as much as her first *Entrepreneur Journeys* despite its being more narrowly focused. It's quite an easy read given that it is essentially a collection of short stories used to illustrate some key insights. For those curious about what makes companies successful, how technology can lead to solutions or perhaps the more specific goal of Mitra - how to 'go to market', *Positioning* delivers."

-*Alan Brochstein, SeekingAlpha/AB Analytical Services blog*

Coming Soon:

Entrepreneur Journeys, Volume Four
Innovation: Need Of The Hour
(Spring 2010)

You can learn more about Sramana Mitra at
www.sramanamitra.com

Online Strategy Roundtables for Entrepreneurs

In addition to her books, Sramana Mitra offers a series of free strategy roundtables for entrepreneurs to address positioning, financing, and other aspects of a startup venture. Up to 1,000 people can attend each session, but only the first five who register to pitch will be able to present their business ideas. All attendees are able to join in on the conversations via a live chat.

You can find more information about these webinars, recordings of past roundtables and registration links to upcoming sessions at:

www.sramanamitra.com/entrepreneurship-strategy-roundtables/

We hope you will join us!

CPSIA information can be obtained at www.ICGtesting.com
Printed in the USA
LVOW07s1954091015

457657LV00029B/871/P